Guide and Indexes to the Conserved and Microfilmed Harris County, Texas Records of Oaths and Allegiance, Declarations of Intent, and Final Naturalizations

1886-1906

By
Robert de Berardinis

Introduction by Robert Schaadt, C.A.
Director, Sam Houston Regional Library

HERITAGE BOOKS
2008

HERITAGE BOOKS

AN IMPRINT OF HERITAGE BOOKS, INC.

Books, CDs, and more—Worldwide

For our listing of thousands of titles see our website
at
www.HeritageBooks.com

Published 2008 by
HERITAGE BOOKS, INC.
Publishing Division
100 Railroad Ave. #104
Westminster, Maryland 21157

The photograph on the cover is the Harris County Courthouse, 1884-1909. This was where all of the
extant Records of Oath and Allegiance, Declarations of Intent, and Records of Final Naturalizations
found in this volume took place and were recorded. The photograph and its digitization were
graciously supplied by Sarah Canby Jackson, C.A., Harris County Archivist.

International Standard Book Numbers
Paperbound: 978-0-7884-4906-2
Clothbound: 978-0-7884-7567-2

Table of Contents

Table of Photographs..iv

Preface v

Acknowledgements vi

Introduction vii

Guide to the Records 1

Key to Cumulative Index................................... 6

Cumulative Index 7

Index to Records of Oaths and Allegiance
    Volume 1 20
    Volume 2 27
    Volume 3 30

Index to Declarations of Intent......................33

Index to Final Naturalizations
    Volume 1 40
    Volume 2 41
    Volume 3 42

Table of Photographs

All digital photographs of documents were imaged by Sarah Canby Jackson, C.A., Harris County Archivist, and with the kind permission of Harris County Clerk Beverly Kaufman

Harris County Courthouse, 1884–1909 ...... cover

Letter regarding Chinese citizenship 4
Found in the Record of Oaths and Allegiance, Volume 2

Record of Oath and Allegiance 19
Found in the Record of Oaths and Allegiance, Volume 2

Declaration of Intent, *first example* 31
Found in Declarations of Intent

Declaration of Intent, *second example* 32
Found in the Record of Oaths and Allegiance, Volume 3

Record of Final Naturalization 35
Petition enlarged detail 36
Affidavit enlarged detail 37
Proof enlarged detail 38
Decree enlarged detail 39
Found in the Record of Final Naturalizations, Volume 1

Preface

The seven volumes that comprise the Harris County Clerk's naturalization records only span a twenty year period, 1886–1906 with a total of 840 pages of records. The remaining records are seemingly lost. The extant records have been properly conserved and microfilmed. This guide and index finding aid completes the archival process. The Records of Oaths and Allegiance comprise three volumes for a total of 563 pages and span from Oct. 27, 1891 to Sept. 28, 1906. The Records of Final Naturalization also comprise three volumes for a total of 137 pages and span from Dec. 4, 1886 to Sept. 25, 1906. There is one volume of Declarations of Intent of 139 pages and it spans from November 1886 through September 1891.

The original indexes for the Records of Oaths and Allegiance and Final Naturalizations can be difficult to use as the spelling is sometimes difficult to read as well as the index giving the incorrect page number. There was no index at for the Declarations of Intent. Included with these indexes is a guide to volumes themselves. On the microfilm, available for purchase from the Harris County Clerk or Interlibrary loan from the Texas State Library, is a citation formula for each volume which is reprinted here:

1. Oath of Allegiance of [Name of Oath Giver], [Date], (Harris County) Record of Oaths and Allegiance, Volume 1, Oct. 27, 1891– Oct. 28, 1896, Harris County Clerk of Court, Houston, Texas. *Oaths of Allegiance and Naturalizations of Harris County, Texas, 1886–1906.* (microfilm edition; Houston, Tex.: Clayton Library Friends, 2005), [Page Number].

2. Oath of Allegiance of [Name of Oath Giver], [Date], (Harris County) Record of Oaths and Allegiance, Volume 2, Oct. 28, 1896– Sept. 28, 1906, Harris County Clerk of Court, Houston, Texas. *Oaths of Allegiance and Naturalizations of Harris County, Texas, 1886–1906.* (microfilm edition; Houston, Tex.: Clayton Library Friends, 2005), [Page Number].

3. Oath of Allegiance of [Name of Oath Giver], [Date], (Harris County) Record of Oaths and Allegiance, Volume 3, Sept. 14, 1903– Sept. 26, 1906, Harris County Clerk of Court, Houston, Texas. *Oaths of Allegiance and Naturalizations of Harris County, Texas, 1886–1906.* (microfilm edition; Houston, Tex.: Clayton Library Friends, 2005), [Page Number].

4. Declaration of [Name of Declarant], [Date], (Harris County) Declarations of Intent, 1886–91, Harris County Clerk of Court, Houston, Texas. *Declarations of Intent of Harris County, Texas, 1886–91.* (microfilm edition; Houston, Tex.: Clayton Library Friends, 2005), [Page Number].

5. Final Naturalization of [Name of New Citizen], [Date], (Harris County) Record of Final Naturalization, Volume 1, Dec. 4, 1886–Oct. 7, 1889, Harris County Clerk of Court, Houston, Texas. *Oaths of Allegiance and Naturalizations of Harris County, Texas, 1886–1906.* (microfilm edition; Houston, Tex.: Clayton Library Friends, 2005), [Page Number].

6. Final Naturalization of [Name of New Citizen], [Date], (Harris County) Record of Final Naturalization, Volume 2, Sept. 6, 1892–Sept. 25, 1906, Harris County Clerk of Court, Houston, Texas. *Oaths of Allegiance and Naturalizations of Harris County, Texas, 1886–1906.* (microfilm edition; Houston, Tex.: Clayton Library Friends, 2005), [Page Number].

7. Final Naturalization of [Name of New Citizen], [Date], (Harris County) Record of Final Naturalization, Volume 3, March 8, 1904–June 6, 1906, Harris County Clerk of Court, Houston, Texas. *Oaths of Allegiance and Naturalizations of Harris County, Texas, 1886–1906.* (microfilm edition; Houston, Tex.: Clayton Library Friends, 2005), [Page Number].

Robert de Berardinis
April 12, 2006

The birthday of my sainted mother Patricia
(Also, the 196th anniversary of Louisiana becoming a state)

Acknowledgements

Even a small volume like this one still requires one to thank a host of people who made it easier. Heading the list is Harris County Clerk Beverly Kaufman and her Deputy Clerk for Administration Dan Sumrall. Their kindness and partnership in allowing the microfilming of a number of their early records has been a very rewarding and enriching experience. Furthermore, the assistance of her archives director Anthony Johnson and his staff of Alejandro "Alex" Moran and Joseph Violante II made this job much easier.

For being the digitally challenged photographer that I am, my grateful thanks to Harris County Archivist Sarah Canby Jackson, C.A., for her kind imaging of the document examples found within. This type of guide is definitely enhanced with the "show and tell" of the documents.

My sincere and heartfelt thanks to Vanessa Smith of the Clayton Library staff. As the microfilm and microfiche manager, she noticed that two of the indexes were difficult to read on the microfilm title, *Oaths of Allegiance and Naturalizations of Harris County, Texas, 1886–1906*. This directly lead to my conclusion that it was easier to make a guide and index than to re-image the microfilm. Then, when the mistakes in the index to the Declarations of Intent were found, it was a serendipitous affirmation of the guide and index project.

I certainly owe a huge thank you to Robert Schaadt, Director of the Sam Houston Regional Library in Liberty for doing the introduction to this guide and index. It was a pleasure to spend many days with him microfilming the Atascosito Archives, the Logan papers, and various records from Jefferson, Orange, and Polk Counties.

Lastly, my thanks to Marje Harris, Clayton Library Manager. It was her desire to build the Texana collection of Clayton Library that lead to the microfilming project that culminated in the preservation of hundreds of volumes and tens of thousands of documents necessary to the documentary history of Texas. This has been a truly once in a lifetime experience thanks to her. It is a debt that I will never be able to repay, but one that future generations of Texans should repay.

R. de B.

Introduction

Immigration and naturalization have been topics of discussion and political debate since the founding of the North American colonies. The legal process of becoming a citizen was rather informal for over 150 years. There was no comprehensive regulation of the naturalization process until Congress passed the Basic Naturalization Act of 1906, establishing the Bureau of Immigration and Naturalization.[1] Congress and the new bureau formulated specific procedures to be followed concurrently by the agency and the courts, encouraging state and local courts to relinquish naturalization cases to the federal courts. Before this, documentation of the naturalization process was sporadic and incomplete.

Prior to 1906 naturalization proceedings took place in any U. S. District Court, in any court of record of the states and/or the Superior or District Courts of the states. In Texas naturalization was entirely handled by its courts of record, primarily the county and district courts, with 95% of the Texas proceedings recorded in the offices of county and district clerk. But the Texas courts of record do include the Justices of the Peace, the County Judge and Commissioners Court, and the county civil, criminal and probate courts.

The filing of the *Declaration of Intent to Become a Citizen* was considered sufficient to obtain the rights of citizenship, to buy land or apply for a land grant and most importantly to prevent from being drafted into the "home country's" military. Draft avoidance explains why the declarations are worded in their specific manner: "It is my bona fide intention, to renounce forever all allegiance and fidelity to any foreign prince, potentate, state, or sovereignty, and particularly to [fill in the blank}." Thus, once the declaration was filed, there was no pressing need to do anything else. Many immigrants to Texas through the port of Galveston appeared in the district court, made their declaration, and moved on to their final destination.

The physical volume of naturalization records dating prior to 1906 is much smaller than one would expect when compared with the Texas immigrant numbers. Some of this can be explained by two factors, many did not bother with the naturalization process and there were several Congressional Amnesty Acts. One of the first Amnesty Acts was granted in 1776 by the Continental Congress when they declared that all people residing in the American Colonies were citizens. Additionally wives and children were covered by the husband's declaration and naturalization papers until 1928. All blacks were not granted citizenship until the 1868 constitutional amendment and Indians or Native Americans were not legally citizens until 1924. The paying of property tax seemed to grant the rights of citizenship and military service with an honorable discharge insured citizenship without any formal petitions.

The Republic of Texas, 1836–1845, specifically stated in its Constitution under the General Provisions, Sec. 6: "All free white persons who shall emigrate to this Republic, and who shall, after a residence of six months, make oath before some competent authority that he intends to reside permanently in the same, and shall swear to support this Constitution, and that he will bear true allegiance to the Republic of Texas, shall be entitled to all the privileges of citizenship." When the Republic of Texas joined the United States of America by treaty in 1845, the U. S. Congress issued a joint resolution that all residents of Texas were granted citizenship.

---

[1] On March 1, 2003, service and benefit functions of the U.S. Immigration and Naturalization Service (INS) transitioned into the Department of Homeland Security (DHS) as the U.S. Citizenship and Immigration Services (USCIS).
http://www.uscis.gov/graphics/aboutus/history/index.htm

Texas naturalization records series include the following titles and descriptions:

1. *Declaration of Intention Record*, 1846. Bound or filed originals or recorded copies of declarations of intention to become citizens filed by aliens with the district court, showing name, age, place of birth, country to which allegiance owed, date and place of arrival, and statement of intention to become a citizen. (Note; until 1952 when filing became optional, aliens had to submit a declaration of intention at least two years prior to applying for naturalization.

2. *Naturalization Papers*, 1846: The following original documents submitted by aliens or their witnesses to the district court in naturalization proceedings or created in the course of those proceedings: *Declaration of Intent, Petitions for Naturalization, Oaths of Allegiance*; *Witness Affidavits, Orders of Court Granting or Denying Citizenship*. These records were incorporated into the *Naturalization Record* in some counties while in others they were maintained in separate files.

3. *Naturalization Record*, 1846. Record of naturalization proceedings held in the district court, showing name of alien, dates of petition and hearing, and orders of court granting or denying rights of citizenship; and which may also include bound-in or recorded copies of petitions, oaths, and affidavits. Often they are found as a separate record, but minutes of naturalization proceedings can be found in the Civil Minutes or the District Court Minutes in many counties, especially before 1869. A separate Naturalization Record relating to minors was created in a few counties.

Not all of these record series were created or maintained in any given county. Often the recording occurred in the court minute books, but it varied according to the clerk's practice, the budget of the office and the offerings of preprinted book sellers. The majority of the local Texas proceedings were recorded in the district court minutes or filed for record in the office of the county clerk, but they may be recorded in any court minute book including criminal or probate minutes. Additionally, the Works Progress Administration workers created indexes to naturalization for many of the Texas counties.

The interesting fact of the WPA indexes is that their range of dates always seem to span longer than the dates for the *Declaration of Intent Record* and the *Naturalization Records* or other extent records. For example, in Harris County the index dates from 1855 to1906 while the declarations date from 1891 to 1906 and the naturalization record dates from 1886 to 1906. In Bexar County the index dates from 1860 to1906 while the declarations date from 1884 to 1892 and the naturalization record dates from 1850 to 1906. In Galveston County the index dates from 1860 to1939 while the declarations found in the county clerk's office date from 1876 to 1906 and the declarations found in the district clerk's office date from 1860 to 1906 and the naturalization record dates from 1886 to 1906. In some instances only the index entry is still extant while the original record cannot be readily found.

In Harris County, naturalization records are found in the offices of the county and district clerk. The following microfilm, expertly described in detail by Robert de Berardinis in this guide, is of the records found in the Office of the County Clerk of Harris County.

Microfilm of the naturalization records from Harris County and other Texas Counties can be ordered for interlibrary loan through the Regional Historical Resource Depository System of the Archives and Information Services Division of the Texas State Library and Archives Commission. The listing is available online at <http://www.tsl.state.tx.us>, click on the Areas of General Interests and then click on Archives and Manuscripts for the direct link.

In 1906 when Congress established the Bureau of Immigration and Naturalization and specified that the federal courts and a few additional courts should have jurisdiction, many Texas

County and District Clerks shipped either their records or part of their records to the federal courts.

Immigration, legal and illegal, has been a topic of heated political discussion since the founding of the nation. It is interesting to note that since 1776 various groups have been identified as being "undesirable" and that their inclusion would ruin the country, and that the impending peril of unlimited immigration would be the downfall of the United States of America, and yet it still stands strong, a nation of diversity and immigrants.

Robert Schaadt, CA
Director,
Sam Houston Regional Library
and Research Center

August 2006
Liberty, Texas

Bibliography

The Texas County Records Manual, Volumes I and Volume II, revised. Austin: Texas State Library and Archives Commission, 1987.

Arlene Eakle and Johni Cerny, eds. *The Source: A Guidebook of American Genealogy.* Salt Lake City: Ancestry Publishing Co., 1984. See chapter 15, "Tracking Immigrant Origins," 452–516.

Sandra M. Burrell, ed. *Texas County Records, A Guide to the Holdings of the Texas State Library of County Records on Microfilm, Depository Edition.* updated edition; Austin: Texas State Library and Archives Commission, 2006. Also, see web site: <http://www.tsl.state.tx.us>. For further information see: the U. S. Immigration and Naturalization Service web site, <http://www.uscis.gov>.

Dedicated to Mary Smith Fay, CG, FASG

My Teacher, Friend, and Yenta

Guide to the Records

The seven volumes comprising the extant "naturalization" records through 1906 held by the Harris County Clerk are of three basic types:

1. Declarations of Intent (1 volume),
2. Oaths and Allegiance (3 volumes), and
3. Final Naturalizations (3 volumes).

All seven volumes were conserved with the pages placed into breathable Mylar sheaths and rebound by 2004 and then microfilmed in 2005. The Declarations of Intent were microfilmed onto 16 mm microfilm and the remaining six volumes were microfilmed onto a single roll of 35 mm microfilm. The two rolls of microfilm can be purchased from the Harris County Clerk or obtained via inter library loan from the Texas State Library and Archives. The two rolls are respectively titled, *Declarations of Intent of Harris County, Texas, 1886–91* and *Oaths of Allegiance and Naturalizations of Harris County, Texas, 1886–1906*.

The Declarations of Intent (to become a naturalized citizen of the United States) span from November 1886 through September 1891. The volume consists of 140 encapsulated pages containing one 6 ½" high x 8 ¼" printed declaration form (or fragments) per page. It is paginated 1–140. Page 138 is blank. Most declarations are either torn or cut. The declarations on pages 3 and 86 are incomplete fragments showing the first name. There is also an additional Declaration found in the beginning of volume 3 of Oaths and Allegiance. The information contained in the Declarations of Intent is as follows:

1. Name of declarant,
2. Country of birth,
3. Current subject or allegiance to what foreign potentate,
4. Age of declarant (in years),
5. Signature of declarant,
6. Date of declaration,
7. Signature of Harris County Clerk, and
8. Signature of Harris County Deputy Clerk.

The three volumes of the Record of Oaths and Allegiance span October 27, 1891 through September 28, 1906. These record the oath given by foreigners to give allegiance to the United States and accept their sovereignty. There is some overlap of the oaths covering same time periods in volumes 2 and 3. All three volumes have two printed forms per page. Volume 1 spans October 27, 1891 through October 28, 1896. It consists of 316 15 ½" high x 10 ½" pages, paginated 1–316 with an original index. The index is missing letters F through L. Volume 2 spans October 28, 1896 through September 28, 1906. It consists of 134 16" high x 10 ¾" pages paginated 1–134 with an original index. During conservation and encapsulation, blank pages 135–140 of volume 2 were removed. Volume 3 spans September 14, 1903 through September 26, 1906. It consists of 14 16" high x 10 ¾" pages paginated 1–14 with an original index. Page 14 is blank. During conservation and encapsulation, an unknown amount of presumably blank pages of volume 3 were removed. They are presumed to be blank pages because the index entries and oaths match. In this volume, as mentioned previously, is a "loose" declaration of intent of September 14, 1903 given by James Bradstreet, the first name in the records of volume 3. The information contained in the Records of Oaths and Allegiance is as follows:

1. Date of Act,
2. Name of Harris County Clerk,
3. Name of oath giver,
4. Native country of oath give,

5. Current subject or allegiance to what foreign potentate,
6. Age of oath giver (in years),
7. Signature of oath giver,
8. Signature of Harris County Clerk, and
9. Signature of Harris County Deputy Clerk.

The three volumes of the Records of Final Naturalization, the record of becoming a naturalized citizen of the United States, span the period from December 4, 1886 through September 25, 1906. There is considerable overlap in time periods covered by each volume. Volume 1 spans from December 4, 1886 through October 2, 1899. It consists of 54 17" high x 10 ½" inch pages paginated 1–54 with an original index. During conservation and encapsulation, blank pages 55–112 of volume 1 were removed. Volume 2 spans September 6, 1892 through September 25, 1906. It consists of 74 16" high x 10 ¾" pages, paginated 1–74 with an original index. During conservation and encapsulation, blank pages 75–336 of volume 2 were removed. Volume 3 spans March 8, 1904 through June 6, 1906. It consists 24 17 ½" high x 11" pages, paginated 1–20 and then paginated 321–324. Pages 8–20 are blank. During conservation and encapsulation, presumably blank pages 21–320 of volume 3 were removed. They are presumed to be blank pages because the index entries and naturalizations match. The information contained in the Records of Final Naturalization is in four parts:

1. Petition,
2. Affidavit,
3. Proof, and
4. Decree.

The information contained within the four parts does vary slightly over the time span. The Petition part generally consists of the following information:

1. Name of petitioner,
2. Native country of petitioner,
3. Date of declaration of intent,
4. Name of county and state that declaration of intent took place,
5. Current subject or allegiance to what foreign potentate (if applicable), and
6. Signature of petitioner.

The Affidavit part generally consists of the following information:

1. Name of petitioner,
2. Current subject or allegiance to what foreign potentate (if applicable),
3. Signature of petitioner,
4. Date of affidavit,
5. Signature of Harris County Clerk, and
6. Signature of Harris County Deputy Clerk.

The Proof part generally consists of the following information:

1. One or two U.S. citizen witnesses,
2. Name of petitioner,
3. Signature of witnesses,
4. Date of Proof supplied,
5. Signature of Harris County Clerk, and
6. Signature of Harris County Deputy Clerk.

The Decree part generally consists of the following information:

1. Date of Decree,
2. Name of petitioner,
3. Native country of petitioner,
4. Current subject or allegiance to what foreign potentate (if applicable), and

5. Signature of Judge (if used).

Finally, there is an interesting historical curiosity in volume 2 of Record of Oaths and Allegiance. It is an August 4, 1900 letter to the Harris County Clerk concerning the "Yellow Peril" of the late nineteenth century—Chinese immigration and citizenship. The letter is from the law firm of Fischer, Sears, and Sherwood, located at the corner of Congress and Main Streets, reminding the clerk that based on an 1882 Federal law (cited in the letter, for which, see photograph, pp. 4–5), no "Chinaman" could be naturalized. There is a rather large body of scholarship on the subject of late nineteenth century Chinese/Asian immigration. Considering that no East Asian names can be found in any of the above seven volumes nor in the companion microfilm title, *Index to Naturalization Records of Harris County District Courts, May 23, 1837–March 5, 1913*, one wonders what the letter was truly addressing. Perhaps a stray Chinese wished to naturalize in Houston, or more likely, someone was imaging that thousands of Chinese were planning to come to Harris County and become naturalized.

HENRY F. FISHER   W. D. SEARS   W. D. SHERWOOD.

Fisher, Sears and Sherwood,

Attorneys and Counselors at Law,

Offices 1, 2, 3, 4 and 5,
WILSON BUILDING.

Corner Main Street
and Congress Avenue.

Houston, Texas, Aug. 4, 1900 189

Mr. E. P. Dupree,

Houston, Texas.

Dear Sir:-

The Act of May 6th, 1882, 47th, Congress, Chapter
126, Section 14, and which appears on page 342, of Vol. 1st,
of the Supplement to the Revised Statutes of the United States,
is as follows:

"That here-after no State Court or Court of the United
States shall admit Chinese to Citizenship, and all laws in con-

Top half of letter regarding Chinese citizenship

4

flict with this act are hereby repealed."

This act is conclusive of the question that a Chinaman can not be naturalized, and this particular section has never been repealed or amended. We have examined all the laws relative to the subject passed by Congress except the acts of the last Congress, which we have not been able to get while investigating this question, but we feel quite positive that the section above referred to was not then amended or repealed.

By virtue of the above Chinaman can not be admitted to citizenship.

Very truly yours,

[signature]

Bottom half of letter regarding Chinese citizenship

Key to Abbreviations Used in Index

DI1 = Declarations of Intent, Nov. 1886–Sept. 1891

FN1 = Final Naturalizations, Volume 1

FN2 = Final Naturalizations, Volume 2

FN3 = Final Naturalizations, Volume 3

OA1 = Oaths and Allegiance, Volume 1

OA2 = Oaths and Allegiance, Volume 2

OA3 = Oaths and Allegiance, Volume 3

Cumulative Index

Abdow, John .... OA3...12
Abdow, John FN3 6
Ackermann, Max .... OA2...44
Adam, Otto OA1.177
Adam, Otto .... FN2 ...67
Adams, Otto .... OA3...10
Addison, James OA2.115
Aebi, Fritz OA2.111
Afrunto, Charles .... OA1...62
Ahmerd, Edward .... OA1...79
Alban, Arthur OA1.262
Alban, Arthur FN3 3
Albarez, Longio OA1.310
Albinus, J. J. .... OA1...54
Alexander, F. .... FN2 ...20
Alias, Estapan .... OA1...33
Alio, Charles OA1.127
Allen, Henry .... OA2...27
Allen, James .... OA2...26
Allen, William .... OA1...90
Allum, Joseph Jr. .... FN1 ...25
Allum, Joseph Jr. .... DI1 ..140
Allum, Joseph Sr. .... FN1 ...24
Alruf, Peter .... OA1...92
Altoffer, J. J. OA1.253
Altorfer, J. C. .... OA2...30
Alwright, Joseph Avery OA1.269
Alwright, W. E. OA1.263
Amann, Jocab .... FN1 ...42
Anderson, August .... OA2...55
Anderson, C. L. OA1.315
Anderson, Charles G. OA1.287
Anderson, E. T. OA1.104
Anderson, John OA1.113
Anderson, Martin OA1.295
André, Francis Adrian .... OA2...28
Angerend, Arter A. OA1.297
Antonietti, Antonio .... OA2...23
Anuwaty, Antoine .... OA2...88
Anuwaty, Butross .... OA2...87
Archer, J. E. OA1.290
Archer, Richard DI1 2
Askew, William .... OA2...89
Ast, M. .... OA1...48
Atkinson, Joseph J. OA1.234
Augoheffer, Robert OA1.198

Austin, W. Y. OA1.169
Baatz, August .... OA1...40
Bafunno, D. D. .... OA1...69
Barnard, Henry .... FN1 ...13
Barwick, J. .... OA2.....6
Bauar, John .... OA3.....1
Baumann, Ernst .... OA2...51
Baumert, Joseph DI1 74
Baziak, John OA1.168
Beaurepaire, Paul .... OA1...71
Becker, Camille Oscar Martin OA1.221
Beer, William OA2.103
Beever "Beaver", George DI1 25
Beleuski, Frank OA1.172
Bender, L. OA1.270
Benignus, John Friederich DI1 53
Benignus, Louis FN1 8
Bening, Heinry "Henry" .... DI1 ..101
Berg, Oscar OA1.250
Bernhardt, Louis .... OA2...50
Bernstein, Lawrence DI1 39
Berthos, Jim OA1.235
Bery, B. OA1.211
Bes Bas, Amos OA1.248
Betis, W. G. .... FN2 ...15
Betts, W. G. .... OA1.....3
Beutel, Ernst .... FN1 ...27
Biderman, A. OA1.283
Biel, George E. .... OA2...73
Bile, Sam OA2.117
Bili, Salvatore OA1.260
Billito, Charles .... OA1...61
Bino, Sam OA1.152
Bisesti, Giacomo OA1.251
Bisesti, Giacomo OA1.251
Black, Max OA1.115
Blaha, Joe .... OA2...22
Blasberg, William .... OA2...61
Blaul, Hermann OA1.207
Bleich, David .... OA1...82
Bliet, Oskar .... DI1 ..134
Blind, Edward OA1.181
Bloom, Israel .... OA2...81
Blouquet, Ed. .... FN2 ...44
Blow, J. H. OA1.303
Blum, Dan OA1.307

Blumenthal, Wm.	**FN2** 8
Blumenthal, Wm.	**FN2** 9
Blunhardt, E. J.	**OA1**.205
Boettcher, Arno	**FN2** ...35
Bogs, Friederich Wilhelm	**DI1** 59
Bogs, Rheinhard Aug.	**DI1** 60
Bohmert, Gustav	**OA1**...96
Bohn, Natan	**OA1**.196
Bolból, Wechebi	**OA1**...31
Bolton, A. J.	**OA2**...78
Bonda, Gusta	**OA1**...27
Bonn, Frank	**OA1**.125
Bonn, Nic	**OA1**.243
Bonna, Frank	**OA1**.242
Borcia, Nic	**OA1**.238
Borgen, Leo	**OA1**.144
Bossolte, Charles	**OA1**.125
Bottler, Paul C.	**OA2**.118
Bottler, Wilhelm	**DI1** 82
Bottler, William	**FN2** ...17
Bowley, J. D.	**OA1**.257
Boysen, A. H.	**FN2** ...11
Bradford, James	**OA3**.....1
Bradshaw, James	**FN1** 9
Brady, Tony	**OA1**...71
Brand, James	**OA1**...98
Braun, Charles	**OA1**.209
Braun, Louis	**OA1**.283
Brennan, John	**FN2** ...32
Brennan, Patrick Joseph	**FN2** ...74
Brennan, Patrick, Joseph	**OA3**...12
Brice, Henry	**OA1**.179
Brill, John	**DI1** 92
Brockler, Victor	**OA2**...82
Brown, E. W.	**OA1**.....3
Brown, Henry	**OA2**...63
Brown, Louis "Lewis"	**OA1**.283
Bruder, Emile	**OA1**.163
Brunna, F.	**OA1**.301
Brunner, Anton	**OA1**.237
Brunner, Anton	**FN2** ...27
Brunner, John	**OA1**.283
Bruno, B.	**OA1**.248
Brusch, Charles	**DI1** 12
Bryan, J. T.	**OA1**...64
Buchholz, F. W.	**OA1**.173
Buchmann, Henrich L. E.	**OA2**...49
Bullai, Gristoforo "Christopher"	**OA1**.150
Burger, George	**OA1**.307
Burger, George	**OA1**.307
Burgheim, D.	**OA1**.219
Bute, James	**OA2**...43
Byrnes, John	**OA1**.....4
Cabis, Debie	**OA1**...26
Cainino, Geordano	**OA1**.254
Canelius, Jim	**OA1**.235
Cannotella, Cosimo	**OA1**.253
Canzona, Dominica	**OA1**.302
Canzoni, Vincenczo	**OA1**.266
Caplund, Herman	**OA1**.203
Caproni, Antonio	**OA1**...91
Caproni, Antonio	**DI1** 23
Carlo, Gulipini	**OA1**...35
Carlo, Gulipini	**FN2** ...24
Carlson, Emile	**OA1**...20
Carlson, G. A.	**OA2**...54
Carson, Dietrich	**OA1**.227
Carter, J. S.	**OA2**...46
Castello, Toney	**OA1**.129
Caulfield, Patrick	**OA1**.226
Cemin, Michael	**DI1** 85
Cherry, Henry	**OA1**.161
Cherry, William	**OA1**.161
Childs, John	**OA1**.111
Christoforos, Paulo	**OA2**.101
Chulla, Joe	**DI1** ..112
Cino, Sampire	**OA1**.151
Ciula, Joe	**OA1**.158
Ciula, Toney	**OA1**.299
Clapp, Walter D.	**OA1**.....2
Clausen, Martin	**OA1**...10
Cliffe, Joe	**DI1** ..102
Clough, Hartwell	**FN1** ...12
Cochins, George	**DI1** ..138
Cohn, Ben	**OA1**.206
Cohn, Sam	**OA1**...76
Coles, Elijah	**DI1** 7
Coles, George	**DI1** 8
Collie, Charles Pain	**OA1**.101
Collie, William	**OA1**...14
Collmorgen, William	**OA1**...76
Connally, Al	**OA1**...19
Connally, Patrick	**OA1**.193
Conway, Daniel	**FN2** ...14
Cooper, George B.	**OA1**.212
Cooper, Thomas B.	**OA2**...90
Cordon, W. T.	**DI1** ..100
Costello, Ancelo	**OA1**.120

Cotrone, Louis................................ OA1.251
Cours, Gaston................................ DI1 ..136
Coyne, Jericho................................ OA1.134
Cracknell, William DI1 62
Craicover, E. .... FN2 ...23
Craicover, Jacob............................ FN2 ...22
Crais, Abraham .... FN1 ...19
Crowe, William .... OA2...29
Crowley, M. D. OA1.228
Crummy, John OA1.249
Cuccia, Frank OA1.150
Cuella, Joe................................ OA1...75
Cuilla, Barthalomew OA1.160
Culon, P.................................... OA1.137
Custis, Joe DI1 15
Damico, Nicolas............................ OA1...15
Damico, Nicolas............................ OA1...17
Damico, Toney............................ OA1.232
Dassmann, Wilhelm........................ OA1...81
Dauna, Carmela............................ OA1.191
Dauna, Charles OA1.152
Davey, Patrick .... OA2...10
David, Richard .... OA1...60
De George, Michela .... OA1...59
De George, Michell .... FN2 ...64
De La Cruz, Guadalupe.................... OA1.201
Debes, John .... OA1...28
Debo, Jorge .... OA1...32
Deebo, Awyn .... OA1...28
Deitzschaed, Paul .... FN2 ...52
Demas, Evan OA1.276
Demmeland, Fred.......................... FN1 ...28
Demopulus, George .... OA3.....4
Demopulus, John.......................... OA3.....5
Deneyelly, A. DI1 11
Diaz, B. OA1.153
Diehl, Anthony............................ DI1 ..105
Diepritio, Thomas OA1.166
Dieseng, Charles .... OA1...85
Dietrich, Emil............................ OA1...47
Dignum, Charles Edward.................. OA1...12
Diliberto, Charles OA1.157
Dolan, John .... OA2...27
Donavan, Dennis............................ OA1...42
Dossman, Herman........................ OA1...38
Drury, Henry .... OA1...86
Dumler, Charles A .... FN1 ...18
Dzierzbicki, Mike.......................... OA1.299
Ebels, Cornelius A. .... OA2...94

Eckert, Joseph .... OA2...10
Eggert, August .... OA2...26
Ehnhardt, Fritz DI1 66
Ehrlund, Charles Axel...................... OA2.126
Eigel, Leonardt Joseph.................... OA2.128
Eldon, Fredrick J. .... FN1 ...11
Elias, Gabriel............................ OA1.258
Elias, Jacob............................ OA1.261
Ellerbrock, Hermann...................... OA1...88
Elliott, David B. .... OA2...66
Emilio, Limido............................ DI1 38
Engelter, Peter............................ DI1 45
Erdmann, H. J............................ OA2...53
Farrerr, Patrick O'D. OA1.136
Farullo, S. OA1.170
Faschon, August............................ OA1...56
Fasula, L. OA1.253
Fasulla, Antonio OA1.153
Fasulla, Frank .... OA1...61
Faure, Theophile .... DI1 ..103
Feely, James OA1.110
Feigelson, Joe............................ OA2...48
Felizola, F. A............................ OA1.240
Feyde, Jaleor .... OA2...36
Fiad, Elias................................ OA1...29
Fiad, Mike .... OA1...31
Ficaro, J. .... OA1...60
Fidele, Deidda "Deida" .... OA2...22
Figlia, Antonio OA1.254
Finke, Charles OA1.304
Finn, E. A. OA1.298
Fischer "Fisher", Emil...................... DI1 18
Fischer, Henry .... OA1...77
Fischer, Jacob .... OA2...42
Fitzgibbons, James........................ OA2.....8
Fitzner, Joe DI1 19
Fitzpatrick, J. A. .... FN1 ...15
Fitzpatrick, John A. DI1 3
Flanagan, James.......................... OA1.175
Flaxman, Max .... OA1...95
Fleishman, Albert OA1.159
Flemele, Charles.......................... OA1...62
Fleutie, Chegolia .... OA1...27
Florian, Leopold.......................... OA1.224
Foley, J. A. OA1.314
Foley, Thomas J. .... OA2.....5
Ford, John P. .... OA2...65
Forgie, John............................ DI1 ..108
Fotis, Ioanis............................ OA2.108

Franco, Dimitre	**OA2**.109	Gloor, Arthur Emil	**OA2**.100
Franek, Josef	**OA1**...72	Goldapper, S.	**OA2**...69
Frank, Henry	**OA1**...85	Goldberg, Charles	**OA1**.190
Frank, Paul	**OA1**.184	Goldblatt, S.	**OA1**.264
Franke, Hermann	**OA1**...97	Goldenberg, Joseph	**OA1**.188
Fraser, William G.	**OA3**.....8	Goldenrath, J.	**OA1**.264
Fred, Peter	**OA2**...19	Goldstein, Charles	**OA1**.139
Freeman, James Dunston	**FN1**...14	Goldstein, P.	**OA1**.187
Frels, John	**OA1**.140	Goldstein, S.	**OA1**.143
French, Herbert Stewart	**OA2**...96	Goldstein, Saal	**OA1**.117
Freund, Henry	**FN1**...20	Gonzales, Cruz	**OA1**.275
Friedlander, Phil	**OA1**.265	Gor[?], Jacob	**DI1**....27
Friedman, I.	**OA1**.289	Gordon, Benjamin	**OA1**.221
Friedman, Joe L.	**OA1**.172	Gourley, Alexander	**OA1**.311
Friedman, L.	**OA1**.187	Gracy, James B.	**DI1**....67
Fry, John James	**DI1**....47	Graham, Lawrence J.	**OA1**.173
Furrer, Henry	**OA1**.213	Greco, Matteo	**OA1**.241
Gadbois, Felix	**OA1**...93	Green, William Joseph	**DI1**....95
Galloway, Robert	**OA1**...63	Greenberg, Barney	**OA1**...90
Gamboa, Jesus	**OA1**.274	Greenberg, Levy	**OA2**...57
Garzo, Tirso	**OA1**.277	Greenberg, Morris	**OA1**...83
Geary, John	**OA1**...55	Greenwood, Thomas	**FN1**...40
Gebbia, Meter	**OA1**.154	Griefferr, Henry	**FN2**...59
Gebbia, Paolo	**OA1**.117	Griffin, Samuel	**OA1**.....1
Gebert, August	**OA2**...46	Griffiths, T. P.	**OA1**...66
Gehring, Fridrich Wilhelm	**OA1**.....1	Gringe, Natale	**OA1**.266
Gennusa, Biagio	**OA1**.301	Grohmann, Joseph	**OA2**...94
George, Charles	**OA1**.223	Gronau, Hermann	**OA1**.280
George, S. F.	**OA1**...33	Grumbach, C.	**FN1**...47
George, Saliba	**OA1**...25	Grünberg, Simon	**OA1**...93
Georges, John	**OA1**...18	Grüner, William	**OA2**...34
Georgio, Bernardo	**OA1**...80	Grunstein, Philipp	**DI1**....77
Gerard, E. V.	**OA1**.105	Gruss, E. W.	**DI1**..118
Gerloff, August	**FN2**...18	Guarino, Domineco	**OA3**.....7
Germanski, Jozef	**OA1**...73	Guarino, Joe	**OA1**.147
Gerstmann, Albert	**OA2**...99	Guiseppe, Guarino	**OA1**.126
Gerstmann, Albert	**OA2**.112	Gunther, F. L.	**OA2**...91
Giametta, Domenico	**OA2**...29	Gurski, Edmund	**OA1**.131
Giarvatano, C.	**OA1**.191	Gussman, Frank	**OA1**...59
Giavatano, Felipe	**OA1**.149	Gutkewsky, Wallace	**OA1**.316
Giaviatario, Charles	**OA1**.136	Guy, E. L.	**FN2**...42
Gibbons, G. A.	**FN1**...23	Gyvanto, Giogi N.	**OA1**.160
Gilbert, Joseph	**OA1**.104	Haas, Hermann	**OA1**.216
Gioccone, G.	2**OA1**.56	Haffa, Jacob	**OA1**...69
Glasberg, Naflate	**OA1**.195	Haley, Martin	**OA1**.105
Glaser, Benjamin	**OA1**.199	Hampe, Albert	**FN1**.....3
Glazar, Stephen	**OA1**...57	Hancock, B. M.	**OA1**.211
Gloger, Anton	**OA1**.109	Hand, James	**OA2**.....7
Gloger, Joseph	**OA1**.113	Hand, Robert	**OA2**.....7

Hanino, Giovanni	OA1.124	Howard, Walter	OA1.185
Hankel, John	FN2 ...43	Hromadka, Frank	OA1.127
Hannsen, Ferdinand	OA2...78	Hueni, Emil	FN1 ...48
Harms, John	OA2...61	Hunkemoller, W. A. C.	OA2...91
Harrison, George	OA1.119	Hunnewall, Charles	FN2 ...54
Harrison, Morris	OA1.306	Hunnewall, Charles	FN1 ...50
Hartman, Eugene	OA2...52	Hurwitz, M.	OA2...11
Hartman, Leopold	OA1.197	Iarosevicz, Johan	OA2...80
Hartmann, Leopold	DI1 99	Ienfeldt, Henry	FN1 ...17
Hartstein, I.	OA2...85	Ignatcza, Kesch	OA1...74
Hauck, Edward Friederich	FN2 5	Ihle, Johann	FN1 6
Hauck, Edward Friedrick	OA1...50	Imhoff, Joseph	DI1 63
Hauer, Edward H.	OA2...18	Ingrando, Ignazio	OA2...57
Havill, George	DI1 28	Iscart, Steinberg	OA1.146
Haynes, Ernest	OA1.141	Issele, Joseph	OA1.292
Hedgecock, F.	DI1 32	Jacob, Forest	OA1.201
Hedgecock, Thomas	DI1 31	Jacobs, David	DI1 22
Hedstrom, John	OA2...37	Jaffroy, George G.	OA1.162
Heibel, Reinhold	OA1...36	Jamail, Assed F.	OA2...86
Heidelberg, Frank	OA1.100	Jamail, Najeib	OA2...87
Heimerdinger, Otto	DI1 ..126	James, Alfred	OA1.149
Hein, John K.	OA2...12	James, William	OA1...95
Heinemann, Carl	OA1...63	Jameson, Joseph	OA1.215
Heinrish, Wilhelm	DI1 94	Janoch, Franz	OA2...32
Heinz, William	OA1.114	Jansen, Karl John	OA1.182
Heise, Albert	OA1...37	Jantz, August	FN1 ...49
Hellberg, Albrecht	OA1...84	Jarvis, George	OA1.142
Helmboy, Frank	OA2...37	Jeffry, Samuel	OA2...99
Herzog, Otto W. H.	OA2...45	Jensen, N. C.	FN2 ...34
Hildebrandt, William	OA2.104	Jensen, Niels Christian	DI1 75
Hill, Cyril C.	OA2.116	Jiuliano, Michele	OA1.249
Hintz, Adolph	OA2...39	John, Abdu	OA1...25
Hluchi, Frank	OA1.103	Johnson, Albert	FN2 ...46
Hochmuth, Carl	FN2 ...51	Johnson, Axel	OA2...20
Hock, Charles J.	OA2.133	Johnson, Carl A.	OA2...68
Hodges, Francis	OA1.119	Jones, Charles	DI1 13
Hodgson, Fred	OA1...42	Jones, Charles M.	OA2...12
Hoffmann, H.	OA1.284	Jorda, John George	FN2 ...60
Hoffmann, Thomas	OA1.225	Jordan, John George	OA1.246
Hollmann, E. H.	OA1.262	Kachis, Cornelius	OA2...34
Holm, Eberhard	FN1 ...36	Kadernoschka, Basta	OA1...89
Holm, Joseph Eric	OA1.289	Kadles, Josef	OA2...13
Holmans, Charles	OA2.107	Kalitta, A. P. J.	FN2 ...10
Holzwarth, George G.	OA2.121	Kaltar, Fan	OA1...23
Hoppe, Fritz	OA2.....5	Kaltar, John	OA1...24
Hoppe, John	OA1.188	Kalter, Betro	OA1...23
Horky, Andy	OA1...89	Kamin, A. H.	OA1...21
Horyates, Petros	OA2.110	Kapner, Isaac	DI1 ..132
Houlihan, John	OA1.228	Kaspar, Jacob	DI1 ..123

Katsimas, Dimetrios........................ 109
Katz, Joel.............................. OA1.183
Kay, John.............................. OA1.138
Kealy, Thomas OA1.302
Kellerson, Thomas B................... OA1.310
Kennedy, John......................... OA1.245
Kennedy, Peter OA1.236
Keough, Martin .... OA1...51
Keough, Martin FN2 6
Kerschwer, P. H. .... OA1...15
Kessler, Hy........................... OA2...74
Kieper, Fred DI1 84
Kifer, R.............................. DI1 ..115
Kill, William Henry .... OA3.....9
Kill, Wm. Henry....................... FN2 ...66
Kirby, Patrick .... OA2...79
Kirsch, Reinhard DI1 51
Kirschmann, Ferdinand................. OA1.199
Kirschnick, A. .... FN1 ...16
Klein, Arthur A. OA1.306
Klein, Henry .... OA1...50
Klein, Hy............................. OA2...73
Kleinkuecht Gottlieb.................. FN2 ...58
Klemppe, Karl "Charles" .... OA2...62
Kliemand, Augustus Bruns Thunig... OA1.....2
Kline, Adolf .... OA1.....3
Klotz, Frederick .... FN1 ...45
Klotz, Isaac.......................... OA1.280
Kluge, Edward .... OA1...30
Knitterscheid, Eugen.................. DI1 ..110
Knitterscheid, Eugene FN2 1
Koehis, Cornelius..................... OA2...34
Koehler, Frank F. OA1.218
Koenig, Andreas....................... DI1 91
König, John DI1 90
Köpke, Edward......................... OA1...30
Kopp, Wilhelm .... OA1...36
Koppel, Joseph........................ OA1...79
Korge, S. Paul OA1.220
Kornpinski, Thomas.................... OA1...46
Korze, J. Paul .... FN2 ...41
Koscher, Edward OA1.198
Kosebe, Otto.......................... OA2...38
Kosler, Frank......................... OA2...71
Krantz, Benjamin DI1 34
Krantz, Jacob......................... DI1 37
Kratzer, Anton........................ OA1.118
Krause, Oscar .... OA2...77
Krischewsky, Rudolph.................. OA1...46

Krischhauser, H....................... OA1.281
Krueger, Celestin DI1 55
Krueger, Otto DI1 50
Kruft, Franz Philip DI1 68
Krynen, Richard OA2.120
Kuhnle, Fritz OA1.278
Kupperman, Isaac...................... DI1 30
Kurbis, Edward OA1.244
Kurbis, Edward .... FN2 ...28
Kurtz, D.............................. OA1...72
Kurz, D............................... DI1 ..117
Kuss, Louis........................... OA1.139
Kutschan, Charles OA1.100
Kutteraff, Eugene .... DI1 ..104
Kutz, Wilhelm OA1.140
Lagrundo, Natizio OA1.305
Lallement, Joseph..................... DI1 10
Lamb, James.......................... OA3.....6
Lamonite, Guiseppe OA1.239
Lamonte, Calagero OA1.237
Lamostu, Calegero OA1.305
Lampiass, Charles OA1.122
Lampiass, Giro .... OA1...16
Lane, William C. FN3 5
Lange, Hans W......................... OA2...21
Langer, Alfred........................ OA2...82
Langer, Vladislav OA2.130
Lardo, John........................... OA1.267
Lassen, Ole .... FN2 ...62
Laughton, Thomas OA2.114
Lavaceo, Jo........................... OA1.268
Lavite, John .... OA1...65
Lavite, John OA1.123
Lawlor, James DI1 83
Lear, Peter DI1 98
Ledergerber, Albert................... DI1 14
Leisner, Fritz .... DI1 ..125
Leith, Charles OA1.102
Leman, Max OA1.131
Lemke, Wilhelm........................ OA1...79
Lemmens, Max.......................... OA1.300
Lenz, Wilhelm......................... DI1 ..124
Leone, Gerone OA2.125
Leone, Ignacio OA1.255
Levenson, G. OA1.130
Levin, Jacob K. DI1 65
Levy, A. T. OA1.279
Lewis, A. .... OA2...44
Lewis, John OA1.258

Lewis, John OA1.258
Lewis, John Bertram .... OA3...13
Lewis, John Bertram .... FN2 ...72
Lichtscheid, Frank.................... OA2...69
Liebig, Arthur........................ OA1.302
Liebowitz, Louis OA1.135
Lieder, Julius........................ FN2 4
Ligatino, Gaetano.................... OA1.145
Ligotino, Francesco Paoli OA1.116
Lindberg, Erick S. .... OA2.....3
Lindsay, John OA1.218
Lininger, Gaston..................... OA2.125
Lipski, Emil.......................... OA1...38
Livingston, M. S. L. OA2.132
Llewellyen, David DI1 4
Lloyd, George .... OA2.....4
Loeser, William...................... FN3 .321
Loesewitz, Erdmann.................. OA2.....9
Loesner, William..................... OA3.....4
Loewen, H. R. .... OA2...34
Loh, Johan Schutte .... OA1...18
Lord, Thomas .... OA2...96
Lorerdi, Antonio..................... OA1.122
Lounay, John George OA1.287
Lowes, Maris......................... OA1.196
Lundquist, Gustaf Adolf .... OA1...82
Lundquist, Oscar OA1.278
Lynch, Dennos OA1.293
Lynch, Jerry OA1.121
Lyons, M. C. .... OA1...11
Lyons, M. J.......................... OA1.158
MacGill, James Campbell .... DI1 ..130
MacGrath, R. H. .... OA2...64
Mack, Heinrich....................... DI1 69
Maeth, Rudolph...................... OA2...79
Maher, Andrew OA1.111
Maher, James OA1.155
Mahne, Fred DI1 88
Mainino, Joe......................... OA1.143
Majorowitz, Albert................... FN3 .323
Majowitz, Stephen OA1.293
Malloy, John......................... FN2 ...55
Malloy, John......................... FN1 ...51
Maltz, A. OA1.164
Malz, Hermann...................... OA2...75
Manas, Charles...................... OA1.236
Mandlomtch, Major OA1.183
Mangelsdorf, Gustave A. OA2.106
Manina, A........................... OA1.195
Mankowski, L. .... FN2 ...57
Mankowski, S....................... OA1.171
Marett, Fred........................ OA1.313
Margiotto, J. OA1.165
Marino, Savario..................... OA1.316
Martens, Peter DI1 64
Martes, Henry J. .... OA2...93
Martin, Fred DI1 6
Martin, Rudolph.................... FN2 ...36
Martinez, Antonio OA1.275
Martinky, Jo OA1.288
Martyr, E. OA1.174
Mascowici, Hiam .... OA1...91
Mason, John Thomas .... OA1...61
Mass, A. OA2.113
Matlage, Franz .... OA1...22
Matzke, Ernst .... DI1 ..137
Mayer, William G. .... OA2...32
McBrady, John Patrick.............. OA2...51
McBurney, William .... OA2...92
McCade, Patrick James .... OA1...48
McCall, Nic........................ OA1.154
McCleary, Hugh.................... OA2...14
McCleary, John OA1.112
McCormack, Charles OA2.115
McDonald, Alfred OA1.288
McDonald, Angus OA1.217
McDonald, John .... OA2.....6
McDonald, John .... OA1...22
McDonald, John .... OA1...22
McDonald, John .... FN2 ...56
McDonald, John .... FN1 ...52
McDougal, Albert OA1.208
McEnroe, J. .... OA2...70
McGinnis, Nicolas .... OA1.....8
McKee, Pete OA1.107
McKing, John...................... OA1.142
McLean, Kenneth OA1.141
McLeary, Joseph OA1.229
Medeo, Jacob OA1.230
Mehl, John......................... OA2.124
Meinscher, Hermann .... OA1...53
Meiselbach, Louis .... DI1 ..129
Melazzo, Leonardo................. OA1...65
Mendlewski, Simon .... OA2...81
Mereles, Santiago.................. OA2...18
Merendino, Joe.................... OA1.259
Merkle, Christ DI1 78
Michelson, Al..................... OA1.245

13

Mikich, Janka L. **DI1** 97
Mill, Peter. **OA3** 3
Miller, C. A. **OA2**.132
Miller, Hyman **OA1**.192
Mills, H. P. **OA1**.130
Mistrula, Joe **OA1**.252
Mogiore, Pietro **OA1**.232
Monkarbel, Jorg .... **OA1**...29
Monspart, John **OA1**.311
Morales, Antonio **OA1**.124
Morales, Giuseppe **OA1**.268
Morales, Matteo **OA1**.151
Moran, P.J. **OA2**.127
Morgenson, Ben .... **OA2**...48
Morgiatta, Angelo **OA1**.238
Möricke, Hermann **OA1**.216
Morrison, Horace .... **OA1**...19
Morrison, Peter. .... **OA3**...11
Morrison, Peter .... **FN2** ...70
Mortensen, Christian .... **OA1**.....9
Moss, M. W. **OA1**.286
Muchow, Max .... **OA2**...62
Mueller, Gustave **FN1** 7
Muldoon, A. A. .... **OA2**...63
Müller, Friederich **FN2** 2
Muller, John .... **FN1** ...41
Müller, Louis **DI1** 36
Murden, L. **OA1**.263
Murray, Robert .... **OA3**.....7
Mustache, Miki .... **OA2**...83
Nagel, H. **OA2**.133
Napoli, Frank **OA1**.135
Napoli, Joe .... **OA1**...66
Naran, Jo **OA1**.243
Nelson, Hans .... **OA1**...98
Neven, Ferdinand .... **FN2** ...16
Newhaus, F. K. .... **FN2** ...19
Neyemes, Sales Tannus .... **DI1** ...16
Neyer, Karl **DI1** 57
Neyland, Edward **OA1**.105
Nikkel; John D. .... **OA2**...33
Nillson, O. W. **OA1**.308
Nitsch, John **OA1**.269
Noack, Max .... **OA1**...67
Noeninger, Gean, Maximin Adelbert **OA1**...39
Norman, L. J. .... **OA2**.....4
Novak, Phillip .... **DI1** ..116
Nugent, John **OA1**.155
O'Brien, D. A. .... **FN2** ...21

O'Meara, John **OA1**.180
O'Meara, William **OA1**.179
Oberholz, Dan **OA2**.117
Oberholz, John **OA1**.197
Oberndorfer, John .... **OA1**...53
Oberpriller, Henry .... **FN1** ...38
Oberpriller, Mathias **DI1** 71
Oelze, Gustave **OA2**.105
Oh, Charles .... **FN1** ...26
Oliver, William **DI1** 24
Olsen, Gustave .... **OA1**.....6
Olson, Ench **OA1**.227
Olsson, Carl .... **OA2**...55
Opperman, Charles William **OA1**.250
Osborne, Joseph .... **OA2**...74
Oslopomik, Ludwig **OA1**.229
Ostermann, John **DI1** 9
Otto, Johann Wilhelm **DI1** 73
Otto, William **DI1** 81
Owen, Patrick .... **FN2** ...73
Owens, Patrick .... **OA3**...13
Page, O. L. .... **OA2**...70
Palemanakas, A. D. **OA1**.231
Palermo, Jo **OA1**.148
Palovich, Charles E. .... **FN2** ...69
Palovitch, Charles E. .... **OA3**...11
Panilla, Ben **OA1**.134
Papayanes, Constantinos .... **OA2**...97
Papdakos, Aristedes .... **OA2**...43
Papyanies, Efatratios **OA2**.101
Parker, H. **OA1**.291
Parker, William .... **OA3**.....9
Parker, William .... **OA2**...71
Parkinson, W. G. .... **OA1**...43
Partillo, Bernardo **OA1**.267
Pasquale, Ciarello **OA1**.147
Patisi, Antonio .... **OA3**.....6
Patterson, William .... **FN2** ...37
Paullemenaker, Peter .... **FN1** ...37
Pavlovich, Charles **OA2**.113
Pawes, John **OA1**.101
Peck, George .... **OA3**.....2
Peine, Charles **OA2**.112
Pell, George W. **OA1**.281
Pellot, Christopher .... **FN2** ...65
Pena, Mauro .... **OA2**...24
Penny, John T. .... **OA1**...35
Perez, E. **OA1**.277
Perez, Thomas **OA1**.274

Perry, James	**FN2**	...13
Peters, William	**OA1**	.176
Peterson, Erik	**OA2**	...47
Peterson, George	**OA1**	...80
Petos, A. Joseph	**OA1**	.272
Pettis, William James	**OA2**	...64
Phelps, Thomas A.	**OA2**	...24
Philip, Panais	**OA2**	.105
Piazzo, Joe	**OA1**	.133
Pietzner, Gottlieb	**FN1**	...31
Pinachia "Panacsea", Frank	**DI1**	..114
Pisch, Joe	**OA1**	...10
Pisch, John	**OA1**	.224
Pizitalas, Vito	**OA1**	.261
Pizzitala, Joseph	**OA1**	.223
Pizzitola, Antonia	**FN2**	...25
Platte, Julius	**FN1**	...29
Platte, W. J.	**FN1**	...34
Pommier, Julius	**OA2**	2
Porter, James	**OA1**	5
Potter, Herbert Ero	**OA2**	...33
Power, John	**FN2**	...53
Power, John A.	**OA1**	.120
Power, W. P.	**OA2**	...15
Praetzel, Wilhelm	**FN1**	...46
Prager, Jacob	**OA3**	3
Prehm, William	**OA2**	...50
Prensky, Sam	**OA2**	.131
Pretswell, John	**OA2**	.121
Pretty, Charles	**OA2**	2
Pretty, Guy	**OA2**	...55
Pretty, Henry	**OA2**	3
Probstle, Joseph	**OA1**	.202
Provenzano, Pasqual	**OA1**	.116
Puccio, Calogero	**OA1**	.256
Pudor, O. M.	**OA1**	.205
Pumpkin, Louis	**OA1**	.176
Purkes, John	**DI1**	54
Quirk, Eugene P.	**OA1**	...21
Rabasti, Pasquale	**OA1**	.261
Radoff, M.	**OA2**	...85
Raff, Adam	**OA1**	...68
Raffael, Paul	**OA1**	.285
Raines, Frank	**OA1**	.163
Ralison, Ezra	**OA1**	.171
Ramano, Aliberto	**OA1**	...34
Rasar, Paul	**OA1**	.108
Rasmitabosky, Edward	**OA1**	...81
Rasmussen, Rasmus N. P.	**OA2**	...67
Rasner, L.	**OA1**	.159
Rattigan, Patrick	**OA1**	.109
Reckwerth, Frank J.	**OA2**	...47
Reichelt, Theodor Edmund	**DI1**	..131
Repsdoreph, Alfred	**OA1**	7
Repsdorph, A	**FN2**	...50
Rethy, Morris	**DI1**	..122
Rheaume, Emére	**DI1**	...20
Ribary, Conrad	**DI1**	...21
Richardson, John	**OA2**	...65
Richardson, John	**FN2**	...61
Rieger, John	**DI1**	...42
Rientlet, Joe	**OA1**	.156
Riley, John	**DI1**	...52
Riordan, M. P.	**OA1**	7
Riske, Samuel	**OA1**	.108
Ritzloff, Otto	**OA1**	.225
Rizziuti, Manano	**OA1**	.137
Roan, William	**DI1**	...44
Robinson, William	**OA2**	...40
Rochat, Edouard "Edward"	**OA2**	...66
Roesler, John	**FN1**	...30
Roffau, Paul	**FN2**	...63
Rogers, Gauci	**OA3**	8
Rohrbach, Ernest Franz	**OA1**	...44
Romano, Alberto	**OA1**	.233
Romano, Alberto	**OA1**	.233
Romano, Antonio	**OA1**	.123
Rommel, Ernst	**DI1**	3
Rooney, William Water	**OA1**	...57
Rose, Gustav William Philip	**FN3**	2
Rose, Gustav William Philip	**FN3**	.322
Rose, Louis	**OA2**	...21
Rosenberg, Ben	**OA2**	.119
Rosenberg, H.	**OA2**	...11
Rosenberg, L.	**OA2**	...68
Rosenberg, L.	**FN3**	4
Rosenthal, Sam	**OA1**	.189
Rothwell, J. H.	**FN1**	...10
Rozzitta, Joseph	**OA1**	.132
Ruby, John H.	**FN1**	...32
Rudnig, Jake	**OA1**	.309
Rudolph, Gustav	**OA2**	...60
Ruff, Friedrick	**FN1**	...44
Ruff, Otto	**OA1**	...70
Ruina, Frank	**OA1**	.260
Russo, Fortunato	**OA1**	...35
Russotto, Guiseppe	**OA2**	1
Ryan, Joseph	**OA2**	...19

Rybicker, Antone .... OA1...20
Sabin, Otto .... OA1...68
Sacks, Israel OA1.167
Sacour, Antonio .... OA1...24
Sadech, John.................................. OA1.213
Saicco, Giocomo OA1.114
Sairka, Stanislas OA1.167
Salavato, Antonio........................... DI1 43
Salem, John.................................... OA1.259
Salim, John.................................... OA1.202
Salim, Joseph J.............................. OA2...88
Salman, Philip OA1.148
Salmeron, Charles OA1.163
Sam, Jake H. OA1.231
Sam, Jake H. .... FN2 ...26
Sam, Jake St. OA1.231
Sanchez, Cesario OA1.276
Sanders, Christian B........................ FN1 1
Sarando, Nalizio............................. OA1.305
Sasi, Josef.................................... DI1 56
Sassie, KennyJ. .... OA1...54
Sauer, Fred OA1.314
Sauer, Venantius August.................... FN1 4
Savage, Arthur George...................... OA1.207
Savage, William OA1.294
Scalio, Ed OA1.285
Scarborough, Thomas Howard .... OA2...92
Scardino, Andria .... OA1...64
Scardino, M. .... OA1...84
Scardino, Vito OA1.156
Schaefer, Hermann.......................... OA2...42
Schall, Frank .... OA1...13
Schalz, John DI1 79
Schalz, Matt "Mathias" DI1 80
Schaper, Henry............................... FN1 ...21
Scheer, Julius DI1 46
Scheiler, Willy OA2.122
Scherman, Leon .... FN1 ...43
Schiel, L. .... OA1...51
Schiel, L. FN2 7
Schiff, Charles............................... OA2.....8
Schiff, H. OA1.315
Schirman, Leon DI1 40
Schlanger, L. OA1.164
Schlock, Charles............................. OA1...13
Schlom, S. .... OA1...73
Schmand, Leonhard DI1 26
Schmidt, Emile............................... OA2...27
Schmidt, Jacob OA2.122

Schmidt, Joe.................................. DI1 76
Schmidt, Louis .... FN1 ...39
Schmidt, Martin FN1 5
Schmidt, Tobois A. .... OA2...35
Schmitz, Julius OA1.178
Schnitzner, J.................................. OA1.210
Schoen, Carl Albert......................... OA1.126
Schoenfeld, Edward OA1.190
Schoom, M. J. OA1.224
Schrader, Hermann.......................... OA2...72
Schuall, Morris .... OA2...14
Schuewolf, Maks............................ OA1.182
Schul, L. .... OA1...51
Schulte, John OA1.200
Schultz, Ast. OA1.184
Schumacher, August OA2.108
Schumacher, F. OA1.204
Schuster, Paul................................ OA1...52
Schutz, Stefen................................ OA2.107
Schwandner, Joe............................. OA1...14
Schwarz, Heinrich........................... DI1 49
Schweinetz, Albert.......................... OA2...38
Scoervuns, James OA1.304
Seery, John J. .... OA1.....2
Sekat, Joseph................................ OA1.303
Semenyak, George OA2.130
Senne, Edward H. F. OA1.177
Seureau, André............................... DI1 ..127
Seureau, George P. E. .... DI1 ..128
Seureau, Paul Gaston .... OA2...58
Shapiro, Max................................. OA2...95
Shapiro, St. OA1.214
Shaughnessy, Michael...................... FN1 2
Sheerine, James .... DI1 ..120
Shepherd, George Fred OA1.271
Shepherd, T. W. DI1 72
Shepherd, William St. OA1.165
Shordloss, Thomas OA1.157
Sievers, Herder P. M. .... OA2...36
Sikesch, Hugo OA1.208
Silbiger, Charles............................. OA1...96
Simon, Elli .... OA1...52
Simon, Harry................................. OA1...12
Simon, Sam .... OA1...99
Sinclair, Neil OA2.104
Singer, Charles OA1.168
Sitto, Friedrick .... OA1...37
Skibell, Abraham .... OA1...77
Skibell, Ramon............................... OA1...74

Smerneos, Deogenes	**OA2**.106	Tamborella, Francisco	**OA1**.128
Smerneos, Keriacos	**OA2**...93	Tamborella, Giovanni "John"	**OA1**.296
Smith, H.	**OA1**.165	Tamburello "Tamborel", Frank	**DI1** ..113
Smith, Jacob H.	**OA2**...35	Tannenberger, Heinerich	**OA2**...72
Smith, Josef	**OA1**.186	Tanner, T. E.	**OA1**...86
Smith, Joseph	**FN2** ...48	Taub, J. H.	**FN2** ...49
Sodich, Jaspar	**OA1**...41	Taub, J. N.	**OA2**...17
Sodich, Pasqual	**OA1**...41	Taub, J. N.	**DI1** ..111
Sodick, Lawrence	**OA1**...58	Taylor, F. A.	**OA1**.185
Southward, W. E.	**OA2**...16	Taylor, F. A.	**FN2** ...39
Sparacio, Argento	**OA1**.194	Tege, William	**OA1**...88
Spegelglas, M.	**OA1**.214	Telge, Louis	**OA1**...49
Spense, A. H.	**OA2**...84	Telge, Louis	**FN2** 3
Speoli, Rudolph	**OA1**.273	Temme, Frederick	**OA1**.271
Spiegel, Albert	**OA1**.241	Temme, Frederick	**FN2** ...30
Spielman, Lewis	**OA1**.279	Tenhoff	**DI1** ....
Spinner, E.	**OA2**...89	Terry, Albert T.	**OA2**.123
Spufero, Leonardo	**OA1**...75	Teska, Friedrich	**DI1** 70
St. Jest, Charles	**OA2**...23	Teske, Fritz	**OA1**.284
Stahl, Louis	**FN1** ...35	Theece, Charles	**OA1**...40
Stall, Joseph	**OA1**.106	Thom, Paul	**OA1**.313
Starkel, Charles	**OA1**.200	Thomas, Ernst	**DI1** 41
Staulberg, Frank	**OA1**...78	Thomas, Joe	**OA2**...59
Stein, Nattan	**OA1**.186	Thomas, John	**OA1**...83
Steinek, Matthew	**FN2** ...40	Thompson, A.	**OA1**...47
Steiner, Math.	**DI1** ..107	Thomsen, Hermann Emil	**OA1**.175
Stentzel, Edward	**OA2**.118	Thomson, Peter Henning	**OA1**.174
Stimpfl, John	**OA2**...52	Thorson, Frank	**OA2**...57
Stipanovich "Stephanus", Vincenzo	**DI1** 17	Tichka, Jacob	**OA2**...13
Stoerkel, Charles John	**FN3** 1	Tobias, Ben	**OA2**...75
Stolz, Hermann F.	**OA2**...40	Tomase, Toney	**OA2**.....1
Stolzenback, George C. W.	**OA2**.129	Tortonau, Tony	**OA2**.120
Stone, A. D.	**OA1**.242	Totarici, Vincenzo	**OA1**.133
Streusand, Harry	**OA1**.295	Traina [?], Charles	**OA1**.129
Stromberg, Frank	**OA1**.291	Traina "Triano", Rocco	**OA1**.247
Stromberg, Frank	**FN2** ...45	Tramonte, Nicolo	**OA1**.170
Strychooski, Martin	**OA1**.312	Tramonte, Nicolo	**OA1**.244
Studhalter, Jost	**OA1**.146	Trania [?], Charles	**OA1**.129
Suarez "Susarez", Carlos	**OA1**.273	Trapolino, Joe	**OA1**.246
Sueba, Abraham	**OA1**.249	Trapolino, John	**OA1**.121
Sullivan, James J.	**OA2**...31	Travieso, Ynez Morales	**OA2**...45
Sullivan, Jerry	**OA1**.286	Treseler, Friederich	**DI1** 58
Sullivan, Richard	**OA1**...94	Trimatore, Solvatore	**OA1**.257
Sundahl, Clarence	**OA1**.222	Trittel, Gustav	**OA1**...45
Suntheim, George	**OA1**...11	Trombatore, K.	**OA1**.297
Sussmann, Theodore L.	**OA2**...56	Turanye, Martin	**OA2**.....9
Swanson, Harry	**OA1**.209	Turley, John	**OA1**.189
Swatloski, John	**OA1**.296	Tyler, Alfred	**OA2**.119
Tamberella, N.	**OA2**...83	Valin, Erik	**OA1**.220

Van der Borgh, J. **OA1**.290

Vartalomartus, Pericles .... **FN2** ...31

Vartalomulus, Pericles **OA1**.281

Vase, Otto.. **OA1**.....8

Vatter, Louis Jr.................................. **OA1**.169

Vetrano, Bernard.............................. **OA1**...97

Vetrano, Joe **OA1**.240

Vetrano, Luigi "Louisi" **OA1**.237

Vinci, Natile..................................... **OA1**.132

Voigt, Chris H.................................. **OA2**...25

Voigt, Julius R,................................. **DI1** 61

Von Harthausen, Hermann................ **DI1** ..106

Waessner, Charles............................ **DI1** 48

Wagner, Louis.................................. **DI1** 29

Wagner, William................................ **FN2** ...47

Walboat, F.. **OA1**.265

Walfort, Sam **OA1**.194

Waljus, Andrew **OA2**.114

Walker, Fred K. Henry....................... **OA2**...30

Wallace, Harry .... **OA1**...58

Walley, James H. **OA1**.144

Walls, William A. **OA1**.180

Walten, George **OA1**.300

Waltrich, Hermann............................ **OA1**.308

Wanke, Will **OA2**.124

Ward, Robert.................................... **OA1**.102

Waslekar, N. N. **OA1**.103

Weber, John .... **OA2**...98

Weber, Paul...................................... **OA2**.127

Wegner, William................................ **DI1** 96

Weidenger, Joe................................. **OA1**.118

Weider, Louis................................... **OA1**...39

Weidneger, Joe.......................see Weidenger

Weil, Hermann.................................. **OA2**...39

Weiner, Isador H. .... **FN1** ...22

Weiner, Isisdore H. .... **DI1** ..121

Weingart, Sam.................................. **OA1**.207

Weiser, John..................................... **OA2**...25

Weiss, Sam....................................... **OA1**.138

Wellenbach, Louis .... **OA2**...15

Wells, George A................................ **OA2**...59

Welrycx "Welricx", Theophile .... **DI1** ..135

Wenck, Charles **OA1**.178

Werthering, H.................................... **FN2** ...38

Westheimer, H. .... **OA1**...94

Westphal, Wilhelm C........................ **OA1**.230

Weyrach, Carl "Charles".................. **DI1** ..109

Whelan, Thomas .... **DI1** ..119

White, Sidney H. .... **OA2**...67

Wicke, Fred...................................... **OA1**.309

Widdig, Gustave............................... **OA1**...87

Wienstroth, Henry............................. **OA1**...56

Wilkenfield, P. **OA1**.216

Wilkers, John **OA1**.219

Wilkins, Charles .... **OA1**...70

Williams, B. **OA1**.115

Williams, William James .... **OA1**...49

Williamson, Cochrane M. **OA2**.123

Willner, Carl Albert .... **OA2**...16

Wilson, Andrew **OA1**.112

Wimmer, Martin................................ **OA1**.181

Wisnerski, Paul **OA1**.292

Witcher, John .... **OA1**...92

Witcher, Thomas............................... **DI1** 89

Wlange, Adolph .... **OA1**...32

Wolff, Johan..................................... **FN2** ...29

Wolff, John....................................... **OA1**.255

Wolff, Oscar..................................... **FN1** ...33

Woodhead, Dave **OA1**.210

Woolsey, Patrick .... **FN2** ...32

Wottrich, Ferdinand **DI1** 86

Wottrich, Herman.............................. **OA3**...10

Wottrich, Hermann............................ **FN2** ...68

Wuderkind, Ludwig **OA1**.203

Wunderlich, Emil **OA1**.192

Wyndelts, M...................................... **OA2**.129

Yanyes, Lander .... **OA1**...87

Yauson, Cy....................................... **OA1**.182

Zallencki, Adam................................ **OA1**.202

Zarth, Herman .... **DI1** ..133

Zeigler, George Adam........................ **DI1** 93

Zerbe, Karl .... **OA2**...98

Zieschang, Herman .... **OA2**...52

Zindler, B. .... **FN2** ...12

Zuber, Aaron **OA1**.222

Zuberber, St...................................... **OA1**.215

Zwink, Adan..................................... **OA1**...43

United States of America.

In County Court.

The State of Texas, } ss.
Harris County.

Be it Remembered, that on this the 5th day of March 19__ before me, _____

E.T. Dupree _____ Clerk of the County Court in and for the State and County aforesaid, personally appeared _____ Aristedes Papadakos _____ and a subject of the King of _____ Greece _____ 25 _____

that he is now residing in the county of Harris aforesaid, that he is _____

_____ the United States, and to renounce forever all allegiance and fidelity to any foreign prince, potentate, state or sovereignty whatever, and particularly to the King _____ of Greece _____

of whom he is now a _____ subject _____

Subscribed and sworn to before me this _____ 5th _____ day of March _____ 19__

_____ Aristedes Papadakos

E.T. Dupree

_____

WITNESS my hand and seal of office at Houston, Texas, this _____ 5 _____ day of March _____ 19__

Record of Oath of Allegiance of Aristedes Pappadakos, volume 2, p. 43

Index to Record of Oaths and Allegiance, Vol. 1

Adams, Otto 177
Afrunto, Charles 62
Ahmerd, Edward 79
Alban, Arthur 262
Albarez, Longio 310
Albinus, J. J. 54
Alias, Estapan 33
Alio, Charles 127
Allen, William 90
Alruf, Peter 92
Altoffer, J. J. 253
Alwright, W. E. 263
Alwright, Joseph Avery 269
Anderson, E. T. 104
Anderson, John 113
Anderson, Charles G. 287
Anderson, Martin 295
Anderson, C. L. 315
Angerend, Arter A. 297
Archer, J. E. 290
Ast, M. 48
Atkinson, Joseph J. 234
Augoheffer, Robert 198
Austin, W. Y. 169
Baatz, August 40
Bafunno, D. D. 69
Baziak, John 168
Beaurepaire, Paul 71
Becker, Camille Oscar Martin 221
Beleuski, Frank 172
Bender, L. 270
Berg, Oscar 250
Berthos, Jim 235
Bery, B. 211
Bes Bas, Amos 248
Betts, W. G. 3
Biderman, A. 283
Bili, Salvatore 260
Billito, Charles 61
Bino, Sam 152
Bisesti, Giacomo 251
Bisesti, Giacomo 251
Black, Max 115
Blaul, Hermann 207
Bleich, David 82
Blind, Edward 181

Blow, J. H. 303
Blum, Dan 307
Blunhardt, E. J. 205
Bohmert, Gustav 96
Bohn, Natan 196
Bolból, Wechebi 31
Bonda, Gusta 27
Bonn, Frank 125
Bonn, Nic 243
Bonna, Frank 242
Borcia, Nic 238
Borgen, Leo 144
Bossolte, Charles 125
Bowley, J. D. 257
Brady, Tony 71
Brand, James 98
Braun, Louis 283
Braun, Charles 209
Brice, Henry 179
Brown, E. W. 3
Brown, Louis "Lewis" 283
Bruder, Emile 163
Brunna, F. 301
Brunner, Anton 237
Brunner, John 283
Bruno, B. 248
Bryan, J. T. 64
Buchholz, F. W. 173
Bullai, Gristoforo "Christopher" 150
Burger, George 307
Burger, George 307
Burgheim, D. 219
Byrnes, John 4
Cabis, Debie 26
Cainino, Geordano 254
Canelius, Jim 235
Cannotella, Cosimo 253
Canzona, Dominica 302
Canzoni, Vincenczo 266
Caplund, Herman 203
Caproni, Antonio 91
Carlo, Gulipini 35
Carlson, Emile 20
Carson, Dietrich 227
Castello, Toney 129
Caulfield, Patrick 226

Cherry, Henry.............................. 161
Cherry, William 161
Childs, John................................. 111
Cino, Sampire.............................. 151
Ciula, Joe.................................... 158
Ciula, Toney................................ 299
Clapp, Walter D. 2
Clausen, Martin 10
Cohn, Sam 76
Cohn, Ben 206
Collie, William............................. 14
Collie, Charles Pain..................... 101
Collmorgen, William 76
Connally, Al 19
Connally, Patrick......................... 193
Cooper, George B. 212
Costello, Ancelo 120
Cotrone, Louis............................. 251
Coyne, Jericho 134
.... 134
Crowley, M. D. 228
Crummy, John 249
Cuccia, Frank 150
Cuella, Joe 75
Cuilla, Barthalomew 160
Culon, P..................................... 137
Damico, Nicolas............................ 15
Damico, Nicolas............................ 17
Damico, Toney............................. 232
Dassmann, Wilhelm........................ 81
Dauna, Charles 152
Dauna, Carmela 191
David, Richard 60
De George, Michela 59
De La Cruz, Guadalupe.................. 201
Debes, John 28
Debo, Jorge 32
Deebo, Awyn 28
Demas, Evan 276
Diaz, B. 153
Diepritio, Thomas 166
Dieseng, Charles 85
Dietrich, Emil................................ 47
Dignum, Charles Edward................. 12
Diliberto, Charles 157
Donavan, Dennis 42
Dossman, Herman 38
Drury, Henry 86
Dzierzbicki, Mike......................... 299

Elias, Jacob................................ 261
Elias, Gabriel.............................. 258
Ellerbrock, Hermann 88
Farrerr, Patrick O'D. 136
Farullo, S................................... 170
Faschon, August............................ 56
Fasula, L.................................... 253
Fasulla, Frank 61
Fasulla, Antonio 153
Feely, James 110
Felizola, F. A.............................. 240
Fiad, Elias................................... 29
Fiad, Mike 31
Ficaro, J..................................... 60
Figlia, Antonio 254
Finke, Charles 304
Finn, E. A. 298
Fischer, Henry.............................. 77
Flanagan, James 175
Flaxman, Max 95
Fleishman, Albert......................... 159
Flemele, Charles........................... 62
Fleutie, Chegolia 27
Florian, Leopold........................... 224
Foley, J. A. 314
Franek, Josef 72
Frank, Henry 85
Frank, Paul 184
Franke, Hermann........................... 97
Frels, John 140
Friedlander, Phil.......................... 265
Friedman, Joe L........................... 172
Friedman, L................................ 187
Friedman, I................................. 289
Furrer, Henry.............................. 213
Gadbois, Felix 93
Galloway, Robert 63
Gamboa, Jesus............................. 274
Garzo, Tirso 277
Geary, John 55
Gebbia, Paolo 117
Gebbia, Meter............................. 154
Gehring, Fridrich Wilhelm................. 1
Gennusa, Biagio 301
George, Saliba.............................. 25
George, S. F. 33
George, Charles........................... 223
Georges, John.............................. 18
Georgio, Bernardo.......................... 80

Gerard, E. V. 105	Heidelberg, Frank.............................. 100
Germanski, Jozef............................. 73	Heinemann, Carl 63
Giarvatano, C. 191	Heinz, William.................................. 114
Giavatano, Felipe 149	Heise, Albert 37
Giaviatario, Charles 136	Hellberg, Albrecht............................. 84
Gilbert, Joseph 104	Hluchi, Frank 103
Gioccone, G. 256	Hodges, Francis................................ 119
Glasberg, Naflate 195	Hodgson, Fred 42
Glaser, Benjamin 199	Hoffmann, Thomas 225
Glazar, Stephen 57	Hoffmann, H. 284
Gloger, Anton.................................. 109	Hollmann, E. H. 262
Gloger, Joseph................................. 113	Holm, Joseph Eric 289
Goldberg, Charles 190	Hoppe, John 188
Goldblatt, S. 264	Horky, Andy.................................... 89
Goldenberg, Joseph 188	Houlihan, John 228
Goldenrath, J. 264	Howard, Walter 185
Goldstein, Saal 117	Hromadka, Frank 127
Goldstein, Charles 139	Ignatcza, Kesch 74
Goldstein, S. 143	Iscart, Steinberg 146
Goldstein, P..................................... 187	Issele, Joseph.................................. 292
Gonzales, Cruz................................. 275	Jacob, Forest................................... 201
Gordon, Benjamin............................ 221	Jaffroy, George G............................. 162
Gourley, Alexander.......................... 311	James, William 95
Graham, Lawrence J. 173	James, Alfred 149
Greco, Matteo.................................. 241	Jameson, Joseph 215
Greenberg, Morris 83	Jansen, Karl John 182
Greenberg, Barney 90	Jarvis, George................................. 142
Griffin, Samuel................................. 1	Jiuliano, Michele.............................. 249
Griffiths, T. P. 66	John, Abdu 25
Gringe, Natale 266	Jordan, John George......................... 246
Gronau, Hermann............................. 280	Kadernoschka, Basta......................... 89
Grünberg, Simon.............................. 93	Kaltar, Fan...................................... 23
Guarino, Joe 147	Kaltar, John 24
Guiseppe, Guarino 126	Kalter, Betro 23
Gurski, Edmund 131	Kamin, A. H. 21
Gussman, Frank 59	Katz, Joel....................................... 183
Gutkewsky, Wallace 316	Kay, John 138
Gyvanto, Giogi N.............................. 160	Kealy, Thomas 302
Haas, Hermann................................ 216	Kellerson, Thomas B......................... 310
Haffa, Jacob 69	Kennedy, Peter................................ 236
Haley, Martin 105	Kennedy, John................................. 245
Hancock, B. M. 211	Keough, Martin 51
Hanino, Giovanni 124	Kerschwer, P. H. 15
Harrison, George.............................. 119	Kirschmann, Ferdinand...................... 199
Harrison, Morris............................... 306	Klein, Henry.................................... 50
Hartman, Leopold 197	Klein, Arthur A. 306
Hauck, Edward Friedrick 50	Kliemand, Augustus Bruns Thunig.......... 2
Haynes, Ernest 141	Kline, Adolf 3
Heibel, Reinhold 36	Klotz, Isaac..................................... 280

Kluge, Edward ... 30
Koehler, Frank F. ... 218
Köpke, Edward ... 30
Kopp, Wilhelm ... 36
Koppel, Joseph ... 79
Korge, S. Paul ... 220
Kornpinski, Thomas ... 46
Koscher, Edward ... 198
Kratzer, Anton ... 118
Krischewsky, Rudolph ... 46
Krischhauser, H. ... 281
Kuhnle, Fritz ... 278
Kurbis, Edward ... 244
Kurtz, D. ... 72
Kuss, Louis ... 139
Kutschan, Charles ... 100
Kutz, Wilhelm ... 140
Lagrundo, Natizio ... 305
Lamonite, Guiseppe ... 239
Lamonte, Calagero ... 237
Lamostu, Calegero ... 305
Lampiass, Giro ... 16
Lampiass, Charles ... 122
Lardo, John ... 267
Lavaceo, Jo ... 268
Lavite, John ... 65
Lavite, John ... 123
Leith, Charles ... 102
Leman, Max ... 131
Lemke, Wilhelm ... 79
Lemmens, Max ... 300
Leone, Ignacio ... 255
Levenson, G. ... 130
Levy, A. T. ... 279
Lewis, John ... 258
Lewis, John ... 258
Liebig, Arthur ... 302
Liebowitz, Louis ... 135
Ligatino, Gaetano ... 145
Ligotino, Francesco Paoli ... 116
Lindsay, John ... 218
Lipski, Emil ... 38
Loh, Johan Schutte ... 18
Lorerdi, Antonio ... 122
Lounay, John George ... 287
Lowes, Maris ... 196
Lundquist, Gustaf Adolf ... 82
Lundquist, Oscar ... 278
Lynch, Jerry ... 121
Lynch, Dennos ... 293
Lyons, M. C. ... 11
Lyons, M. J. ... 158
Maher, Andrew ... 111
Maher, James ... 155
Mainino, Joe ... 143
Majowitz, Stephen ... 293
Maltz, A. ... 164
Manas, Charles ... 236
Mandlomtch, Major ... 183
Manina, A. ... 195
Mankowski, S. ... 171
Marett, Fred ... 313
Margiotto, J. ... 165
Marino, Savario ... 316
Martinez, Antonio ... 275
Martinky, Jo ... 288
Martyr, E. ... 174
Mascowici, Hiam ... 91
Mason, John Thomas ... 61
Matlage, Franz ... 22
McCade, Patrick James ... 48
McCall, Nic ... 154
McCleary, John ... 112
McDonald, John ... 22
McDonald, Angus ... 217
McDonald, Alfred ... 288
McDonald, John ... 22
McDougal, Albert ... 208
McGinnis, Nicolas ... 8
McKee, Pete ... 107
McKing, John ... 142
McLean, Kenneth ... 141
McLeary, Joseph ... 229
Medeo, Jacob ... 230
Meinscher, Hermann ... 53
Melazzo, Leonardo ... 65
Merendino, Joe ... 259
Michelson, Al ... 245
Miller, Hyman ... 192
Mills, H. P. ... 130
Mistrula, Joe ... 252
Mogiore, Pietro ... 232
Monkarbel, Jorg ... 29
Monspart, John ... 311
Morales, Antonio ... 124
Morales, Matteo ... 151
Morales, Giuseppe ... 268
Morgiatta, Angelo ... 238

Möricke, Hermann	216
Morrison, Horace	19
Mortensen, Christian	9
Moss, M. W.	286
Murden, L.	263
Napoli, Joe	66
Napoli, Frank	135
Naran, Jo	243
Nelson, Hans	98
Neyland, Edward	105
Nillson, O. W.	308
Nitsch, John	269
Noack, Max	67
Noeninger, Gean, Maximin Adelbert	39
Nugent, John	155
O'Meara, William	179
O'Meara, John	180
Oberholz, John	197
Oberndorfer, John	53
Olsen, Gustave	6
Olson, Ench	227
Opperman, Charles William	250
Oslopomik, Ludwig	229
Palemanakas, A. D.	231
Palermo, Jo	148
Panilla, Ben	134
Parker, H.	291
Parkinson, W. G.	43
Partillo, Bernardo	267
Pasquale, Ciarello	147
Pawes, John	101
Pell, George W.	281
Penny, John T.	35
Perez, Thomas	274
Perez, E.	277
Peters, William	176
Peterson, George	80
Petos, A. Joseph	272
Piazzo, Joe	133
Pisch, Joe	10
Pisch, John	224
Pizitalas, Vito	261
Pizzitala, Joseph	223
Porter, James	5
Power, John A.	120
Probstle, Joseph	202
Provenzano, Pasqual	116
Puccio, Calogero	256
Pudor, O. M.	205
Pumpkin, Louis	176
Quirk, Eugene P.	21
Rabasti, Pasquale	261
Raff, Adam	68
Raffael, Paul	285
Raines, Frank	163
Ralison, Ezra	171
Ramano, Aliberto	34
Rasar, Paul	108
Rasmitabosky, Edward	81
Rasner, L.	159
Rattigan, Patrick	109
Repsdoreph, Alfred	7
Rientlet, Joe	156
Riordan, M. P.	7
Riske, Samuel	108
Ritzloff, Otto	225
Rizziuti, Manano	137
Rohrbach, Ernest Franz	44
Romano, Alberto	233
Romano, Alberto	233
Romano, Antonio	123
Rooney, William Water	57
Rosenthal, Sam	189
Rozzitta, Joseph	132
Rudnig, Jake	309
Ruff, Otto	70
Ruina, Frank	260
Russo, Fortunato	35
Rybicker, Antone	20
Sabin, Otto	68
Sacks, Israel	167
Sacour, Antonio	24
Sadech, John	213
Saicco, Giocomo	114
Sairka, Stanislas	167
Salem, John	259
Salim, John	202
Salman, Philip	148
Salmeron, Charles	163
Sam, Jake H.	231
Sam, Jake St.	231
Sanchez, Cesario	276
Sarando, Nalizio	305
Sassie, Kenny J.	54
Sauer, Fred	314
Savage, William	294
Savage, Arthur George	207
Scalio, Ed	285

Scardino, Andria 64
Scardino, M. 84
Scardino, Vito 156
Schall, Frank 13
Schiel, L. 51
Schiff, H. 315
Schlanger, L. 164
Schlock, Charles 13
Schlom, S. 73
Schmitz, Julius 178
Schnitzner, J. 210
Schoen, Carl Albert 126
Schoenfeld, Edward 190
Schoom, M. J. 224
Schuewolf, Maks 182
Schul, L. 51
Schulte, John 200
Schultz, Ast. 184
Schumacher, F. 204
Schuster, Paul 52
Schwandner, Joe 14
Scoervuns, James 304
Seery, John J. 2
Sekat, Joseph 303
Senne, Edward H. F. 177
Shapiro, St. 214
Shepherd, William St. 165
Shepherd, George Fred 271
Shordloss, Thomas 157
Sikesch, Hugo 208
Silbiger, Charles 96
Simon, Harry 12
Simon, Elli 52
Simon, Sam 99
Singer, Charles 168
Sitto, Friedrick 37
Skibell, Ramon 74
Skibell, Abraham 77
Smith, H. 165
Smith, Josef 186
Sodich, Jaspar 41
Sodich, Pasqual 41
Sodick, Lawrence 58
Sparacio, Argento 194
Spegelglas, M. 214
Speoli, Rudolph 273
Spiegel, Albert 241
Spielman, Lewis 279
Spufero, Leonardo 75

Stall, Joseph 106
Starkel, Charles 200
Staulberg, Frank 78
Stein, Nattan 186
Stone, A. D. 242
Streusand, Harry 295
Stromberg, Frank 291
Strychooski, Martin 312
Studhalter, Jost 146
Suarez "Susarez", Carlos 273
Sueba, Abraham 249
Sullivan, Richard 94
Sullivan, Jerry 286
Sundahl, Clarence 222
Suntheim, George 11
Swanson, Harry 209
Swatloski, John 296
Tamborella, Francisco 128
Tamborella, Giovanni "John" 296
Tanner, T. E. 86
Taylor, F. A. 185
Tege, William 88
Telge, Louis 49
Temme, Frederick 271
Teske, Fritz 284
Theece, Charles 40
Thom, Paul 313
Thomas, John 83
Thompson, A. 47
Thomsen, Hermann Emil 175
Thomson, Peter Henning 174
Totarici, Vincenzo 133
Traina [?], Charles 129
Traina "Triano", Rocco 247
Tramonte, Nicolo 170
Tramonte, Nicolo 244
Trania [?], Charles 129
Trapolino, John 121
Trapolino, Joe 246
Trimatore, Solvatore 257
Trittel, Gustav 45
Trombatore, K. 297
Turley, John 189
Valin, Erik 220
Van der Borgh, J. 290
Vartalomulus, Pericles 281
Vase, Otto 8
Vatter, Louis Jr. 169
Vetrano, Bernard 97

Vetrano, Luigi "Louisi" 237
Vetrano, Joe 240
Vinci, Natile 132
Walboat, F. 265
Walfort, Sam 194
Wallace, Harry 58
Walley, James H. 144
Walls, William A. 180
Walten, George 300
Waltrich, Hermann 308
Ward, Robert 102
Waslekar, N. N. 103
Weidenger, Joe 118
Weider, Louis 39
Weidneger, Joe .... see Weidenger
Weingart, Sam 207
Weiss, Sam 138
Wenck, Charles 178
Westheimer, H. 94
Westphal, Wilhelm C. 230
Wicke, Fred 309
Widdig, Gustave 87

Wienstroth, Henry 56
Wilkenfield, P. 216
Wilkers, John 219
Wilkins, Charles 70
Williams, William James 49
Williams, B. 115
Wilson, Andrew 112
Wimmer, Martin 181
Wisnerski, Paul 292
Witcher, John 92
Wlange, Adolph 32
Wolff, John 255
Woodhead, Dave 210
Wuderkind, Ludwig 203
Wunderlich, Emil 192
Yanyes, Lander 87
Yauson, Cy 182
Zallencki, Adam 202
Zuber, Aaron 222
Zuberber, St. 215
Zwink, Adan 43

Index to Record of Oaths and Allegiance, Vol. 2

Ackermann, Max 44
Addison, James 115
Aebi, Fritz 111
Allen, Henry 27
Allen, James 26
Altorfer, J. C. 30
Anderson, August 55
André, Francis Adrian 28
Antonietti, Antonio 23
Anuwaty, Antoine 88
Anuwaty, Butross 87
Askew, William 89
Barwick, J. 6
Baumann, Ernst 51
Beer, William 103
Bernhardt, Louis 50
Biel, George E. 73
Bile, Sam 117
Blaha, Joe 22
Blasberg, William 61
Bloom, Israel 81
Bolton, A. J. 78
Bottler, Paul C. 118
Brockler, Victor 82
Brown, Henry 63
Buchmann, Henrich L. E. 49
Bute, James 43
Carlson, G. A. 54
Carter, J. S. 46
Christoforos, Paulo 101
Cooper, Thomas B. 90
Crowe, William 29
Davey, Patrick 10
Dolan, John 27
Ebels, Cornelius A. 94
Eckert, Joseph 10
Eggert, August 26
Ehrlund, Charles Axel 126
Eigel, Leonardt Joseph 128
Elliott, David B. 66
Erdmann, H. J. 53
Feigelson, Joe 48
Feyde, Jaleor 36
Fidele, Deidda "Deida" 22
Fischer, Jacob 42
Fitzgibbons, James 8

Foley, Thomas J. 5
Ford, John P. 65
Fotis, Ioanis 108
Franco, Dimitre 109
Fred, Peter 19
French, Herbert Stewart 96
Gebert, August 46
Gerstmann, Albert 99
Gerstmann, Albert 112
Giametta, Domenico 29
Gloor, Arthur Emil 100
Goldapper, S. 69
Greenberg, Levy 57
Grohmann, Joseph 94
Grüner, William 34
Gunther, F. L. 91
Hand, James 7
Hand, Robert 7
Hannsen, Ferdinand 78
Harms, John 61
Hartman, Eugene 52
Hartstein, I. 85
Hauer, Edward H. 18
Hedstrom, John 37
Hein, John K. 12
Helmboy, Frank 37
Herzog, Otto W. H. 45
Hildebrandt, William 104
Hill, Cyril C. 116
Hintz, Adolph 39
Hock, Charles J. 133
Holmans, Charles 107
Holzwarth, George G. 121
Hoppe, Fritz 5
Horyates, Petros 110
Hunkemoller, W. A. C. 91
Hurwitz, M. 11
Iarosevicz, Johan 80
Ingrando, Ignazio 57
Jamail, Assed F. 86
Jamail, Najeib 87
Janoch, Franz 32
Jeffry, Samuel 99
Johnson, Axel 20
Johnson, Carl A. 68
Jones, Charles M. 12

Kachis, Cornelius 34
Kadles, Josef 13
Katsimas, Dimetrios 109
Kessler, Hy 74
Kirby, Patrick 79
Klein, Hy 73
Klemppe, Karl "Charles" 62
Koehis, Cornelius.............................. 34
Kosebe, Otto.................................... 38
Kosler, Frank 71
Krause, Oscar 77
Krynen, Richard 120
Lange, Hans W. 21
Langer, Alfred 82
Langer, Vladislav 130
Laughton, Thomas 114
Leone, Gerone 125
Lewis, A. 44
Lichtscheid, Frank............................. 69
Lindberg, Erick S. 3
Lininger, Gaston................................ 125
Livingston, M. S. L. 132
Lloyd, George 4
Loesewitz, Erdmann............................ 9
Loewen, H. R. 34
Lord, Thomas 96
MacGrath, R. H. 64
Maeth, Rudolph................................. 79
Malz, Hermann.................................. 75
Mangelsdorf, Gustave A. 106
Martes, Henry J................................. 93
Mass, A. 113
Mayer, William G. 32
McBrady, John Patrick......................... 51
McBurney, William 92
McCleary, Hugh................................ 14
McCormack, Charles 115
McDonald, John 6
McEnroe, J. 70
Mehl, John....................................... 124
Mendlewski, Simon 81
Mereles, Santiago............................... 18
Miller, C. A. 132
Moran, P.J. 127
Morgenson, Ben 48
Muchow, Max 62
Muldoon, A. A. 63
Mustache, Miki 83
Nagel, H. 133

Nikkel; John D. 33
Norman, L. J..................................... 4
Oberholz, Dan 117
Oelze, Gustave 105
Olsson, Carl..................................... 55
Osborne, Joseph 74
Page, O. L. 70
Papayanes, Constantinos..................... 97
Pappadakos, Aristedes 43
Papyanies, Efatratios.......................... 101
Parker, William 71
Pavlovich, Charles 113
Peine, Charles................................... 112
Pena, Mauro 24
Peterson, Erik 47
Pettis, William James.......................... 64
Phelps, Thomas A. 24
Philip, Panais................................... 105
Pommier, Julius................................. 2
Potter, Herbert Ero 33
Power, W. P. 15
Prehm, William 50
Prensky, Sam.................................... 131
Pretswell, John 121
Pretty, Charles.................................. 2
Pretty, Guy 55
Pretty, Henry 3
Radoff, M. 85
Rasmussen, Rasmus N. P...................... 67
Reckwerth, Frank J. 47
Richardson, John............................... 65
Robinson, William 40
Rochat, Edouard "Edward"..................... 66
Rose, Louis...................................... 21
Rosenberg, Ben 119
Rosenberg, H.................................... 11
Rosenberg, L. 68
Rudolph, Gustav................................ 60
Russotto, Guiseppe............................. 1
Ryan, Joseph 19
Salim, Joseph J.................................. 88
Scarborough, Thomas Howard 92
Schaefer, Hermann............................. 42
Scheiler, Willy 122
Schiff, Charles................................... 8
Schmidt, Emile.................................. 27
Schmidt, Jacob 122
Schmidt, Tobois A. 35
Schrader, Hermann............................. 72

Schuall, Morris 14
Schumacher, August 108
Schutz, Stefen.. 107
Schweinetz, Albert 38
Semenyak, George 130
Seureau, Paul Gaston 58
Shapiro, Max.. 95
Sievers, Herder P. M. 36
Sinclair, Neil 104
Smerneos, Deogenes 106
Smerneos, Keriacos 93
Smith, Jacob H. 35
Southward, W. E. 16
Spense, A. H... 84
Spinner, E.. 89
St. Jest, Charles 23
Stentzel, Edward 118
Stimpfl, John 52
Stolz, Hermann F. 40
Stolzenback, George C. W.................... 129
Sullivan, James J. 31
Sussmann, Theodore L........................... 56
Tamberella, N... 83
Tannenberger, Heinerich....................... 72
Taub, J. N. 17
Terry, Albert T. 123

Thomas, Joe 59
Thorson, Frank....................................... 57
Tichka, Jacob 13
Tobias, Ben 75
Tomase, Toney.. 1
Tortonau, Tony...................................... 120
Travieso, Ynez Morales 45
Turanye, Martin 9
Tyler, Alfred... 119
Voigt, Chris H. 25
Waljus, Andrew 114
Walker, Fred K. Henry........................... 30
Wanke, Will 124
Weber, John 98
Weber, Paul 127
Weil, Hermann.. 39
Weiser, John... 25
Wellenbach, Louis 15
Wells, George A...................................... 59
White, Sidney H...................................... 67
Williamson, Cochrane M. 123
Willner, Carl Albert 16
Wyndelts, M.. 129
Zerbe, Karl 98
Zieschang, Herman 52

Index to Record of Oaths and Allegiance, Vol. 3

Abdow, John 12
Adams, Otto 10
Bauar, John 1
Bradford, James 1
Brennan, Patrick, Joseph 12
Demopulus, George 4
Demopulus, John 5
Fraser, William G. 8
Guarino, Domineco 7
Kill, William Henry 9
Lamb, James 6
Lewis, John Bertram 13

Loesner, William 4
Mill, Peter 3
Morrison, Peter 11
Murray, Robert 7
Owens, Patrick 13
Palovitch, Charles E. 11
Parker, William 9
Patisi, Antonio 6
Peck, George 2
Prager, Jacob 3
Rogers, Gauci 8
Wottrich, Herman 10

THE STATE OF TEXAS,
HARRIS COUNTY.

I, _Friederich Tresler_ being duly sworn [or affirmed], according to law, declares and says that he is a native of _Germany_ and a _citizen_ of the _city_ of _Minden_ ; that he is now residing in the county of Harris aforesaid; that he is **38** years of age, or thereabouts, and that it is _bona fide_ his intention to become a citizen of the United States, and to renounce forever all allegiance and fidelity to any foreign prince, potentate, state, or sovereignty whatever, and particularly to the _Emperor_ of _Germany_ of whom he is now a _subject_ —

Friederich Tresler

Sworn to and subscribed before me this **18** day of _Oct_ 18 **88**

Alex Erichson
Clerk C. C. H. C.

By _Alex Vaughlingah._
Deputy.

Declaration of Intent, *first example*, from Declarations of Intent, p. 58

31

THE STATE OF TEXAS,

County of _Harris_ } _County_ Court.

Before me, the undersigned authority, on this day personally appeared _James Bradford_ who declares upon oath that he is the natural born subject of _the King of Great Britain Ireland_; that he was born in _England_; that he is _Galveston_ _Texas_ years of age; that he emigrated to the United States of America and arrived at the port of _Galveston Texas_ on or about the _7_ day of _____ in the State of _Texas_ 190_3_; that it is his _bona fide_ intention to become a citizen of the United States, and renounce forever all allegiance and fidelity to any foreign Prince, Potentate, State Sovereignty whatsoever, and particularly my and all allegiance to the _King of Great Britain Ireland_ and that he will bear true allegiance to the United States, and support the Constitution and laws of the same, and that he does not disbelieve in, nor is he opposed to all organized government; nor is he a member of or affiliated with any organization entertaining or teaching such disbelief in or opposition to all organized government; nor does he, or any association to which he belongs, advocate or teach the duty, necessity or propriety of the unlawful killing of any officer or officers generally of the government of the United States, or of any other organized government, because of his or their official character; nor has he violated any of the provisions of the Act of Congress entitled "An Act to regulate the emigration of aliens into the United States," approved March 3, 1903.

James Bradford

Subscribed and sworn to before me, this _14_ day of _Sept_ 190_3_

Witness my hand and seal of office, at _Houston Texas_ this _Sept_ day of _Sept_ 1903

E. T. Kupien Clerk
County Court, Harris County.

By _R. Kennedy_ Deputy.

I hereby certify that the above is a true copy of the original, taken from the records of the _____ Court of said County.

Witness my hand and seal of office, at _____ this _____ day of _____ 190_.

_____ Clerk
_____ Court, _____ County.

By _____ Deputy.

Declaration of Intent, *second example*, from Oaths and Allegiance, vol. 3, p. 1

Index to Declarations of Intent

Allun, Joseph Jr. 140
Archer, Richard 2
Baumert, Joseph 74
Beever "Beaver", George 25
Benignus, John Friederich 53
Bening, Heinry "Henry" 101
Bernstein, Lawrence 39
Bliet, Oskar 134
Bogs, Friederich Wilhelm 59
Bogs, Rheinhard Aug. 60
Bottler, Wilhelm 82
Brill, Joh. 92
Brusch, Charles 12
Caproni, Antonio 23
Cemin, Michael 85
Chulla, Joe 112
Cliffe, Joe 102
Cochins, George 138
Coles, Elijah 7
Coles, George 8
Cordon, W. T. 100
Cours, Gaston 136
Cracknell, William 62
Custis, Joe 15
Deneyelly, A. 11
Diehl, Anthony 105
Ehnhardt, Fritz 66
Emilio, Limido 38
Engelter, Peter 45
Faure, Theophile 103
Fischer "Fisher", Emil 18
Fitzner, Joe 19
Fitzpatrick, John A. 3
Forgie, John 108
Fry, John James 47
Gor[?], Jacob 27
Gracy, James B. 67
Green, William Joseph 95
Grunstein, Philipp 77
Gruss, E. W. 118
Hartmann, Leopold 99
Havill, George 28
Hedgecock, F. 32
Hedgecock, Thomas 31
Heimerdinger, Otto 126
Heinrish, Wilhelm 94

Imhoff, Joseph 63
Jacobs, David 22
Jensen, Niels Christian 75
Jones, Charles 13
Kapner, Isaac 132
Kaspar, Jacob 123
Kieper, Fred 84
Kifer, R. 115
Kirsch, Reinhard 51
Knitterscheid, Eugen 110
Koenig, Andreas 91
König, John 90
Krantz, Benjamin 34
Krantz, Jacob 37
Krueger, Celestin 55
Krueger, Otto 50
Kruft, Franz Philip 68
Kupperman, Isaac 30
Kurz, D. 117
Kutteraff, Eugene 104
Lallement, Joseph 10
Lawlor, James 83
Lear, Peter 98
Ledergerber, Albert 14
Leisner, Fritz 125
Lenz, Wilhelm 124
Levin, Jacob K. 65
Llewellyen, David 4
MacGill, James Campbell 130
Mack, Heinrich 69
Mahne, Fred 88
Martens, Peter 64
Martin, Fred 6
Matzke, Ernst 137
Meiselbach, Louis 129
Merkle, Christ 78
Mikich, Janka L. 97
Müller, Louis 36
Neyemes, Sales Tannus 16
Neyer, Karl 57
Novak, Phillip 116
Oberpriller, Mathias 71
Oliver, William 24
Ostermann, John 9
Otto, Johann Wilhelm 73
Otto, Wm. 81

Declarations of Intent

Pinachia "Panacsea", Frank	114	Shepherd, T. W.	72
Purkes, John	54	Steiner, Math.	107
Reichelt, Theodor Edmund	131	Stipanovich "Stephanus", Vincenzo	17
Rethy, Morris	122	Tamburello "Tamborel", Frank	113
Rheaume, Emére	20	Taub, J. N.	111
Ribary, Conrad	21	Tenhoff	140
Rieger, John	42	Teska, Friedrich	70
Riley, John	52	Thomas, Ernst	41
Roan, William	44	Treseler, Friederich	58
Rommel, Ernst	3	Voigt, Julius R.,	61
Salavato, Antonio	43	Von Harthausen, Hermann	106
Sasi, Josef	56	Waessner, Charles	48
Schalz, John	79	Wagner, Louis	29
Schalz, Matt "Mathias"	80	Wegner, William	96
Scheer, Julius	46	Weiner, Isisdore H.	121
Schirman, Leon	40	Welrycx "Welricx", Theophile	135
Schmand, Leonhard	26	Weyrach, Carl "Charles"	109
Schmidt, Joe	76	Whelan, Thomas	119
Schwarz, Heinrich	49	Witcher, Thomas	89
Seureau, André	127	Wottrich, Ferdinand	86
Seureau, Geo. P. E.	128	Zarth, Herman	133
Sheerine, James	120	Zeigler, George Adam	93

PETITION.

THE STATE OF TEXAS. } COUNTY COURT. *Janry* TERM, 18*89*

HARRIS COUNTY. } *J A Fitzpatrick* respectfully shows

To the Honorable County Court of said County

that he is a native of *Ireland* ; that on the day of

A.D. 18*83* . before the Clerk of the *County* Court of *Harris* County, State of

Texas he declared on oath that it was *bona fide* his intention to become a citizen of the

United States, and to renounce forever all allegiance and fidelity to any foreign prince, potentate, state or sovereignty whatever, and particularly to the *Queen* of *Great Britain*

of whom he was at that time a *Subject* ; that he has resided within the United States upwards of five

years, and in the State of Texas one year, both periods immediately preceding this his application to become a

citizen of the United States, and that he has never borne any hereditary title, or been of any of the orders of

nobility, in his own or any other country. He therefore prays that, on his making proof and taking the oath

prescribed by law, he may be admitted a citizen of the United States of America *J A Fitzpatrick*

AFFIDAVIT.

I *J A Fitzpatrick* do swear [or affirm] that the contents of the foregoing petition are

true; that I will support the Constitution of the United States, and I now renounce and relinquish any title or

order of nobility to which I am now or may be hereafter entitled, and I do absolutely and entirely renounce and

abjure all allegiance and fidelity to any foreign prince, potentate, state or sovereignty whatever, and particularly

to the *Queen* of *Great Britain* of whom I was before a *Subject*

J A Fitzpatrick Sworn to and subscribed in open court this *10th*

day of *Janry* A.D. 18*89* *J S Massie*

{L.S.} Clerk of the County Court, Harris County, Texas

By *S N Stamford* Deputy

PROOF.

A B Anderson and *E N Vaemer* citizens of the United States of America being duly sworn [or

affirmed] according to law, saith that he knows and is well acquainted with *J A Fitzpatrick*

the petitioner, that to his knowledge he has resided in the United States five years, and in the State of Texas one

year, both periods immediately preceding his application to become a citizen, that during the said period of five

years he has behaved as a person of good moral character, attached to the principles of the Constitution of the

United States, and well disposed to the good order and happiness of the same. *E N Vaemer*

A B Anderson Sworn to and subscribed in open Court this *10th*

day of *January* A.D. 18*89* *J S Massie*

{L.S.} By *S N Stamford* Deputy

DECREE.

UNITED STATES OF AMERICA. } THE STATE OF TEXAS } ss.
COUNTY OF HARRIS }

BE IT REMEMBERED, that at the County Court for the County of Harris aforesaid, held at the court house

thereof, in the city of Houston, on the *10th* day of *January* A.D. 18*89*

J A Fitzpatrick a native of *Ireland* exhibited a petition,

praying to be admitted to become a citizen of the United States, and it appearing to the Court that he had declared

on oath [or affirmation] before the Clerk of the *County* Court in and for the *County* aforesaid

on the day of A.D. 18*83*, that it was *bona fide* his intention to become

a citizen of the United States, and to renounce forever all allegiance and fidelity to any foreign prince, potentate,

state, or sovereignty whatsoever, and particularly to the *Queen* of *Great Britain*

of whom he was at that time a *Subject* ; and the said *J A Fitzpatrick*

having on oath declared, and also made proof thereof, agreeably to law, to the satisfaction of the Court, that he

had resided one year and upwards within the State of Texas, and within the United States of America upwards of

five years, both periods immediately preceding his application, and that during said period of five years he had

behaved as a man of good moral character, attached to the principles of the Constitution of the United States,

and well disposed to the good order and happiness of the same, and having declared on oath [or affirmation]

before the said Court that he would support the Constitution of the United States, and that he did absolutely and

entirely renounce and abjure all allegiance and fidelity to every foreign prince, potentate, state and sovereignty

whatsoever, and particularly to the *Queen* of *Great Britain* , of whom he was

before a *Subject* , and having in all respects complied with the laws in regard to naturalization;

Thereupon the said Court admitted the said *J A Fitzpatrick* to become a citizen of

the United States, and ordered all the proceedings aforesaid to be entered in the records of said Court.

Record of Final Naturalization of J. A. Firzpatrick, from vol. 1, p. 15

Enlarged detail of Petition portion of Final Naturalization of J. A. Fitzpatrick

Enlarged detail of Affidavit portion of Final Naturalization of J. A. Fitzpatrick

PROOF

A. R. Andrews and E. M. Warner X citizens of the United States of America being duly sworn (or affirmed), according to law, each that he knows and is well acquainted with J. A. Fitzpatrick the petitioner; that to his knowledge he has resided in the United States five years, and X the State of Texas one year, both periods immediately preceding his application to become a citizen; that during the said period of five years he has behaved as a person of good moral character, attached to the principles of the Constitution of the United States, and well disposed to the good order and happiness of the same.

A. R. Andrews

E. M. Warner

Sworn to and subscribed in open Court this 10th day of January A.D. 18 87

[L.S.]

By J. Wren

J. N. Fitzpatrick

Enlarged detail of Proof portion of Final Naturalization of J. A. Fitzpatrick

38

UNITED STATES OF AMERICA.

THE STATE OF TEXAS } ss.
COUNTY OF HARRIS }

DECREE

BE IT REMEMBERED, that at the County Court for the County of Harris aforesaid, held at the court house thereof, in the city of Houston, on the 10th day of January A.D. 1889, *J. A. Fitzpatrick* a native of _____ exhibited a petition, praying to be admitted to become a citizen of the United States, and it appearing to the Court that he had declared on oath [or affirmation] before the Clerk of the *County* Court in and for the *County* aforesaid on the _____ day of _____ A.D. 188 3, that it was *bona fide* his intention to become a citizen of the United States, and to renounce forever all allegiance and fidelity to my foreign prince, potentate, state, or sovereignty whatsoever, and particularly to the *Queen* of *Great Britain* and the said *Subject* of whom he was at that time a *Subject*, and the said *J. A. Fitzpatrick* to the satisfaction of the Court, that he having on oath declared, and also made proof thereof, agreeably to law, that during said period of five years he had had resided one year and upwards within the State of Texas, and within the United States of America upwards of five years, both periods *immediately* preceding his application, and that during said period of five years he had behaved as a man of good moral character, attached to the principles of the Constitution of the United States, and well disposed to the good order and happiness of the same, and having declared on oath [or affirmation] before the said Court that he would support the Constitution of the United States, and that he did absolutely and entirely renounce and abjure all allegiance and fidelity to every foreign prince, potentate, state and sovereignty whatsoever, and particularly to the *Queen* of *Great Britain*, of whom he was before a *Subject*, and having in all respects complied with the laws in regard to naturalization: Thereupon the said Court admitted the said *J. A. Fitzpatrick* to become a citizen of the United States, and ordered all the proceedings aforesaid to be entered in the records of said Court.

Enlarged detail of Decree portion of Final Naturalization of J. A. Fitzpatrick

39

Index to Record of Final Naturalization, Vol. 1

Allum, Joseph Jr. 25
Allum, Joseph Sr. 24
Amann, Jocab 42
Barnard, Henry 13
Benignus, Louis 8
Beutel, Ernst 27
Bradshaw, James 9
Clough, Hartwell 12
Crais, Abraham 19
Demmeland, Fred 28
Dumler, Charles A 18
Eldon, Fredrick J. 11
Fitzpatrick, J. A. 15
Freeman, James Dunston 14
Freund, Henry 20
Gibbons, G. A. 23
Greenwood, Thomas 40
Grumbach, C. 47
Hampe, Albert 3
Holm, Eberhard 36
Hueni, Emil 48
Hunnewall, Charles 50
Ienfeldt, Henry 17
Ihle, Johann 6
Jantz, August 49
Kirschnick, A. 16

Klotz, Frederick 45
Malloy, John 51
McDonald, John 52
Mueller, Gustave 7
Muller, John 41
Oberpriller, Henry 38
Oh, Charles 26
Paullemenaker, Peter 37
Pietzner, Gottlieb 31
Platte, Julius 29
Platte, W. J. 34
Praetzel, Wilhelm 46
Roesler, John 30
Rothwell, J. H. 10
Ruby, John H. 32
Ruff, Friedrick 44
Sanders, Christian B. 1
Sauer, Venantius August 4
Schaper, Henry 21
Scherman, Leon 43
Schmidt, Louis 39
Schmidt, Martin 5
Shaughnessy, Michael 2
Stahl, Louis 35
Weiner, Isador H. 22
Wolff, Oscar 33